MODERN ANIMALISM
Habitats of Scarcity and Wealth in Comics and
Literature

Modern Animalism

Habitats of Scarcity and Wealth in Comics and Literature

GLENN WILLMOTT

UNIVERSITY OF TORONTO PRESS
Toronto Buffalo London

© University of Toronto Press Incorporated 2012
Toronto Buffalo London
www.utppublishing.com
Printed in Canada

ISBN: 978-1-4426-4317-8

Printed on acid-free

Library and Archives Canada Cataloguing in Publication

Willmott, Glenn, 1963–
Modern animalism : habitats of scarcity and wealth in comics
and literature / Glenn Willmott.

Includes bibliographical references and index.
ISBN 978-1-4426-4317-8

1. Primitivism in literature.   2. Economics in literature.   3. Ecology
in literature.   4. Scarcity.   5. Modernism (Literature).
6. Postmodernism (Literature).   I. Title.

PN56.P7W54 2012   809'.911   C2012-900751-X

The University of Toronto Press acknowledges the financial assistance
to its publishing program of the Canada Council for the Arts and the
Ontario Arts Council.

 Canada Council   Conseil des Arts   ONTARIO ARTS COUNCIL
for the Arts   du Canada   CONSEIL DES ARTS DE L'ONTARIO

This book has been published with the help of a grant from the
Canadian Federation for the Humanities and Social Sciences, through
the Aid to Scholarly Publications Program, using funds provided by
the Social Sciences and Humanities Research Council of Canada.

University of Toronto Press acknowledges the financial support of
the Government of Canada through the Canada Book Fund for its
publishing activities.

Art remains loyal to humankind uniquely through its inhumanity in regard to it.
Theodor Adorno, 1969

In a thousand years, electively mutated post-humans will look back at us with awe and wonder. They'll say that this was when humans and the planet got married, fused, melted together, the moment when one could no longer separate the two. I hope they see that we did it with a sense of humour.
Douglas Coupland, 2010

Contents

Acknowledgments

I am grateful to Yaël Schlick for introducing me to Krazy Kat, who started me on this journey, as well as for her unerring literary and critical sense approaching its end, during the book's revisions. I am also indebted to my students at Queen's University for engaging with my interest in graphic narratives and extending my knowledge of them. The project has been nurtured over the years by the community gathered by the annual conference of the Modernist Studies Association, while Philip Armstrong and colleagues at the University of Canterbury, at which I was a visiting fellow under the Erskine Programme in 2010, hosted me during its completion. Special thanks are also due Siobhan McMenemy for her greatly appreciated editorial support at UTP, and to the insightful critical commentaries of three anonymous reviewers. This research project was carried out with the aid of a grant from the Social Sciences and Humanities Research Council of Canada.

MODERN ANIMALISM
Habitats of Scarcity and Wealth in Comics and
Literature

Introduction

You face a square of transparent glass hemmed in by immutable black walls. Within its depths of clear glass flow delicate translucent blobs, rings of luminous membrane alive with a languid self-exposure. Reaching, touching, contracting, hanging in space, they secrete startling effects of colour and imperceptible motion. They slide over and against each other, or face each other, in static, pregnant emptiness as you face them. Something tugs at you, the pull exerted by pictures of life, but here without any recognizable face or form. Is it because these small, radiant figures evoke a memory of cellular plasm under microscope glass, or of protozoan life adrift in its watery layers? We know we are made of something like this. We even know that in a court of law, something akin to this, the blobby genetic substance of our cells, is what identifies us absolutely, so that we cannot escape recognition, a face we cannot darken or turn aside. But these images are paint, and explicitly painting effects; there is no illusionistic subterfuge. Beside the black box the artist, Rui Pimenta, has placed a printed title that reads as a caption: *that subtle knot which makes us human* (see colour plate 1). So it is not a window, but a mirror. Nearby, a kindred scene embedded in glass bears the caption: *my soul takes limbs of flesh*.[1] You would not be mistaken, then, to recognize an image of creaturely life here, indeed of human life – and a moment of silent, gorgeous human contact, however microbiotic, in these psychedelic raindrops. As such, they are not quite realist reflections, nor are they arbitrary signs. In this strange iconic world, we recognize our own or another 'I.' What makes this possible? How you or I could imagine such identification – unthinkable in like terms a hundred or more years ago – is the subject of this book. There is more to it than the ability to recognize oneself in representations of a common animal life or spiritual core of some non-human life. That capacity is archaic, and its humanist expression, which Shakespeare imagined as an emotional life, sympathy foremost, that would make us strange bedfellows with what looks to be monstrous, has a long modern heritage.[2] Pimenta's protozoan figures are the end point of a more recent heritage beginning with modernism, in which human form and identity have been rendered radically plastic, simultaneously in language and visual depiction. It has less to do with sympathy or other sentiment, I will argue, than with style. In any case, its *subjective* challenge is, I trust, now familiar to us – to re-imagine human and individual identity as traversing racial, animal, gender, and technological categories, rather than organizing them invisibly from above, in favour of somebody's power and status.

The latter, hierarchical view is the lesson of another painting, Diego Velázquez's *Las Meninas* (1656), famously studied by Michel Foucault as a wily, spatial unfolding of the assumptions of anthropocentric representation – of the sovereign human subject manufactured and concealed at the heart of Enlightenment knowledge.[3] While Foucault does not discuss style, it is consistent with his argument that the painting is elaborately illusionistic; it erases its own iconography as such, and offers a transparent effect of the real. Compare with this a painting offering a similar play of sightlines, mirrors, and subjects in a studio, which is just as manifestly about representation itself, yet foregrounds a stylized iconography: Paul Gauguin's *Te Rerioa* (The Dream), which he made in Tahiti in 1897 (see colour plate 2). Gauguin's painting, and his re-invention of style, will offer us a starting point here, to trace the modernist heritage that will give birth to Pimenta's plasmatic mirrors. There is an *objective* side to this re-imagining of the human figure, too, and I will suggest that the subjective challenge is its by-product: it is a new kind of economic vision, prompted at first by modernist ennui with bourgeois life, and subsequently by the postmodern revelation of limits to natural resources and life-sustaining ecology, a vision in which habitat is grasped and represented according to animal relations and values at odds with modern conventions of wealth and scarcity. When I encountered Pimenta's work, it was gathered under the title *Living within the Means of Existence*, and the exhibition's tableaus were as much mirrors of the self as they were mirrors of habitat, a seduction to strange expressions of wants and resources. So, too, are Gauguin's paintings efforts, not only to confound and transfigure spectators' idea of themselves as human, but of what their environment has to offer them, of wealth itself as an end to life.

In *Te Rerioa*, we see none of the natural growth or landscape of Tahiti so abundant in Gauguin's other paintings, except in a further representation. Partly visible behind two seated women, a baby in a decoratively carved cradle, and a reclining cat, are two unframed paintings, one relatively conventional, of a horse and rider in a tropical landscape, the other more frieze-like and symbolist, of a figure half human, half lotus flower, standing above procreating rabbits, simplified trees in the background. Beside the women, child, and cat runs a strip of decorative mosaic pattern along the floor, which the cat appears to be observing, and a painted mural that fills the wall with sequences of animals, plants, and metamorphic humans. Unlike to the taut chiasmus structure that Foucault finds in *Las Meninas*, this painting is off-balance, without a centre of gravity: your gaze cascades from one figure to another, real or painted. The woman on the right looks directly out at us, while the woman in the precise centre, but a bit behind her, looks off to the right at what to us remains invisible; behind the central woman, on the wall, a butterfly woman looks the opposite direction, as if mirroring her; so too does a child carved on the cradle below her. Only the eyes of the sleeping child are closed, revealing nothing. In this particle chamber of gazes and transformations, what holds us is neither the sovereignty of our own gaze (which is merely abused by the welter of sightlines rebounding across the human, the animal, the iconographic, and the invisible) nor the recognition of face (whose mask-like stylization anticipates, like the murals themselves, the cartoon iconography of modern comics). These 'dream' faces appear in a metamorphic continuum across the painting, from sketchily realistic, to increasingly iconic and animal.

If we did not accept the implication of our own non-anthropomorphic reflection in the scene, we would have to accept that of the painter, who represents himself (doubly) in the carved and the sleeping child – the child of which woman we do not know, but clearly a nurtured member of this whole human-animal kin grouping and the iconographic medium (the 'dream') which is its habitat. On the cradle, noticeably above the lower border of the painting and in three lines fitted to the cradle's back, so that the words are themselves cradled by the body of the carved child with open eyes, in a jumble of capital and lower-case roman lettering and cursive script (so that writing is insistently a graphical element on the same continuum), is the triple naming, 'TE RERIOA / P Gauguin 97 / TAITI.' The artist identifies with the child, born of Tahiti and its lives, represented here as a real world as plastic and synthetic as a dream. Gauguin recognizes in this painting the emergence of his own genealogical identity – so far as he becomes rooted in a new ecology, both human and non-human, that determines how he will see and name himself – that can only be rendered in a strange, new kind of iconology. He thus figures himself a child of the Eve figure of *Te nave nave fenua* (The Delightful Land) of 1892, a polydactylic woman based at least partly on a Javanese temple figure and partly on a Tahitian model, which art historian Stephen Eisenman has described in style and symbology as 'neither desirable nor repellent, neither Tahitian nor European, neither classical nor modern, neither black nor white, neither Venus nor chimpanzee and neither originative nor degenerate.'[4] To identify with her child – for Gauguin, a figure of uncharacteristic modesty and vulnerability – is to identify with the contingency of historical kindred as much as with an avant-gardist's freedom to dream. Between these two polarities, modernism will explore the human as a problem creature, and its habitat as a place of ambiguous violence and welfare. My insistence on habitat and its representation is deliberate; in using the word 'habitat,' I will be referring to environments that sustain a creature or creatures in a given historical situation, whether shaping or shaped by non-human natural systems or human economies of consumption and production. A central proposition of this book is that modernity should be understood as a geo-historical panoply of such habitats, of which the various (anthropocentric) evocations of social and historical contexts that have normally grounded the interpretation of art and literature, along with purely environmentalist perspectives, are so many fragments. The story I want to tell will move from the figure of the modern habitat towards the figure of the problem creature that it makes possible; in so doing, it will shuttle between the origins of these figures in modernism and their efflorescence in the present.

Modernism was once heard as the voice of an age, of a modernity thought to reveal its full indeterminacies and potentialities for personal and social life in the years leading up to the First World War, and to encompass a human condition whose fragility and violence, hopes and fears, would subtend like tectonic plates the surface histories of a long twentieth century. Yet, though many of us still turn to writers of this age for insight or renewal of perspective upon our lives today, we may no longer fully recognize the human condition of which they were long thought to have spoken – neither its coherence nor its universality. From its inception, the cultural field of high art and avant-garde modernisms upon which a literary canon and disciplinary community were founded has been entangled with the production of ideologies of modernism. As this field recedes into the past and becomes an historical period – a contested turning point and event, rather than climax and agency in the loose narrative of literary history – the field more readily discloses its diversity and incoherence, its polyphonies as well as its silences, before what remains to be imagined. If modernism once spoke, now modernisms echo. These modernisms are an inheritance, a heritage to be understood genealogically in relation to, rather than as an expression of, what has now become the modern.

One silence that must divide us from the artists of the early twentieth century and estrange us from their heritage, which could hardly be more profound, concerns the perception and experience of scarcity. These have undergone a sea change. Is there enough oil and water? Are air and sunlight pathogenic? What happens as our population grows? Ours is a small planet: we are shocked into repression or agitation when we contemplate its walls. Theirs, however, was an open planet; they were bewildered or allured by the casting open of doors, for good or ill. Even the Great Depression was more of a battleground for competing ideas of property and its distribution, than for alternative ideas of abundance itself. Both our and their visions remain true, perhaps, but difficult to hold in perspective together. Everywhere we turn today, we are reminded of the material unsustainability of our present way of life as a global species and, indeed, of the modern itself as we have inherited this concept in a set of economic institutions and lifestyle values and expectations in the industrialized West and beyond. We are haunted by the finite, not merely as a local situation, but as a horizon. Such a condition was hardly imaginable to the earlier literary avant-garde or to their publics. Then as now, scarcity was an historical and political construct, a thing of human making and unmaking. The actual planetary resources – the natural capital – out of which scarcity or its opposite experience, abundance, was manufactured were rarely distinguished as a problem for human life or its representation. A signal exception, H.G. Wells's vision of a bleak, post-human future in *The Time Machine* (1895), proves the rule, for it has been remembered more for its dystopian class allegory than for the inhospitable, inhuman, and finally uninhabitable planet into which these historical classes and their species must vanish.

On the contrary, literary scholars agree that the modernist

age was ruled by an ideology and experience of abundance, beyond which any scarcity could only be an experience produced by power imbalances or ascetic refusal. This is the theme of Ronald Schleifer's study of the 'post-Enlightenment world of abundance,' which argues that abundance 'characterizes the problem of the new century in the arts and sciences.' He quotes the influential modernist economist John Maynard Keynes's view, expressed in 1931, that 'from the sixteenth century,'

> with a cumulative crescendo after the eighteenth, the great age of science and technical inventions began, which since the beginning of the nineteenth century has been in full flood – coal, steam, electricity, petrol, steel, rubber, cotton, the chemical industries, automatic machinery and the methods of mass production, wireless, printing, Newton, Darwin, and Einstein, and thousands of other things and men too famous and familiar to catalogue,

and tells us that Keynes predicted that technological change in the past decade or two had been so great that the human species might look forward to having all its material needs satisfied without burdensome labour or conflict, and that 'man will be faced with his real, his permanent problem' of defining values and activity proper to a new realm of freedom. This technological utopia is a familiar, if now quaintly obsolete vision; yet it figures as a commonplace among both intelligentsia and the wider publics of Keynes's day. Modern abundance is a product of unbridled technological power and scientific knowledge. For Schleifer, it is reflected stylistically in the 'multiplication of voices' by James Joyce, the 'multiplication of rhythms' by Igor Stravinsky, and the 'multiplication of planes' by Pablo Picasso.[5]

Such liberation of traditional form to multiplications of excess may be telling, but even those artists concerned with poverty and constriction of wealth, such as (very diversely) Ezra Pound and Virginia Woolf, produced an aesthetics of abundance rooted in this same Enlightenment utopia. Alec Marsh has detailed how Pound, like William Carlos Williams, dedicated himself and his poetry to a Distributist political economy because he believed that the core problems of economic inequity lay solely in the distribution of modern goods, not their means of production or resource base. Pound wanted thus to represent and to 'reestablish an economy of abundance' whose material and natural basis he took – like his mentor Dante, who idealized a timeless, natural economy – already to be there, and whose industrial infrastructure and tremendous productive powers – unlike to Dante's time – he accepted; for him, the enemy is not industrialization, but the irresponsible new agency behind it, the competitive corporation.[6] The arcana of Pound's and Williams's engagements with Social Credit may deter one from recognizing the wider currency of their assumptions about the fundamental abundance achieved by modernizing societies. What they shared with others was a belief that the crisis in modern abundance, the cause of modern economic inequalities and ensuing political and social troubles, lay in the accumulation and hoarding of wealth as capital, as a primary economic goal.

As Michael Tratner has shown, this diagnosis is at the heart of Keynes's own prescription for modern society, which was to increase wealth by increasing the circulation of value and goods via increased consumption – meaning, for the common person as for the state, to make a virtue of saving less and spending more. In Tratner's reading, post–First World War culture valorizes and normalizes a deficit spending approach to wealth and property that an earlier generation stigmatized as unhealthy or dissolute. And this new ideology of expenditure is reflected in the content and form of modernist writing. Tratner shows the connections between them in a reading of Virginia Woolf's work. He quotes Stuart Chase's *The Economy of Abundance* (1934), which denounces the hoarding of 'surplus' by a financial elite and urges its distribution to the consumer for expenditure, echoing Pound on the need for state control of money and markets, but emphasizing the individual's 'moral duty' to consume. Tratner observes that Woolf's *Three Guineas* (1938) 'is an unusual variation of such an abundance theory,' as the 'whole essay is about how to use what she calls "surplus funds," the three guineas she can give away. Her central indictment of the current economic system is that men use the surpluses they have to pursue increased surpluses instead of devoting them "to education, to pleasure, to philanthropy."'[7] He goes on to read *Mrs. Dalloway* (1925), itself evidently readable as a kind of scandalous freedom of psychological and narrative dilation, wandering, and ephemeral aesthetic effects, as asserting just such surplus expenditures of mind, body, and property against practices of exclusion and restraint. He finds a similar ideology of expenditure – founded on a belief in a repressed, or uneven, modernity of abundance – in a wide range of writers from Joyce to Zora Neale Hurston. So it appears that Mrs Dalloway is ahead of her time, able to distract us from 'pseudo-moral principles which have hag-ridden us for two hundred years,' as Keynes writes of his utopia free of material scarcity, and able to 'teach us how to pluck the hour and the day virtuously and well.'[8]

Yet there is something counter-intuitive in all of these lines of argument, when it comes to modernists and their art. Did Woolf, Joyce, Pound, Hurston, and others merely join the crowd in expressing, however more engagingly or idiosyncratically, a regnant bourgeois ideology of abundance? Is the widespread personal or principled refusal of ethical conventions based on aims and logics driven by the marketplace, if not a sham, a bald contradiction? On the contrary, this study will argue that unless one distinguishes between differing economic forms of abundance and modes of scarcity, all modernist production will blend into homologous abstractions, only differentiable in situation and effect, rather than in structure and purpose. One should not risk losing sight of what this study will view as the most important aspect of the modernist inheritance for us today – the diverse imagination of modes of living that strictly refuse the modern ideologies of abundance and which, clothed in startling images of impoverishment and scarcity, re-imagine abundance itself. That work is more crucial today than any modernist was able to foresee. Nor is it lost on contemporary writers, those who awoke to the crisis of a planet getting smaller rather than larger.

What is abundance? One thinks naturally of the cornucopia of goods: material necessities and comforts, those which satisfy needs and desires in a proximal, accessible swarm around the individual, from bread to sitting rooms to cell phones. Beyond this we may immediately add a whole range of intangible goods and services in relation to health, education, vocational options, and pastoral care. Perhaps we include environmental conditions such as unpolluted water and air, or state apparatuses such as constitutional rights that allow for expansion of individual life opportunities and expression. The idea of economic abundance is limited only to any good, service, or condition produced by economic activity – or, to put it another way, to any satisfaction of a need or desire in which economic activity determines the nature of that satisfaction. Economic activity simply refers to the total range of production, distribution, exchange, and ownership of valued, material or intangible things and capacities. It requires only a little thought to see that economic abundance as such is the commonsensical aim – and in liberal ideology, perhaps the utopian ideal – to which the more currently powerful notion of economic 'development' refers, encompassing not only a growth in goods and services, but also a growth in general welfare. Modern ideologues of abundance did not found their utopian assumptions solely on a proliferation of things to buy and the wherewithal to buy them, but also on a vision of humanity free to replace the horrors of national and class conflict with more genuinely satisfying, pleasurable ends for human activity: an invitation to realize one's own version of Mrs Dalloway's party.

Abundance, then, refers to different kinds of economic activity and the production and reproduction, for a common person, of satisfying environments of valued things and capacities, or wealth. Different kinds of abundance are usefully implicated in four distinct modes of wealth creation, or growth, identified by the environmental economist Paul Ekins:

1 The growth in physical throughput of the economy (measured in physical units of matter and energy)

2 The growth of the production of the economy (measured in monetary value units, conventionally by GDP and GNP)
3 The growth in human welfare (whose method of measurement remains controversial)
4 The growth of biomass, as part of natural process (measured in physical units)

These categories of growth correspond to four kinds of production to which I will apply the following terminology:

1 HABITAT PRODUCTION: the making and remaking of the human and non-human, material and biological environment in which human life is embedded
2 CONSUMER PRODUCTION: the making of goods and services for utility or consumption
3 WELFARE PRODUCTION: the making and remaking of satisfying life experiences or conditions
4 NATURAL PRODUCTION: the human and non-human processes of growth and change

Recent economic interpretations of modernist literary production, discussed above, have assimilated modernism to consumer production, a market-based understanding of abundance in which excessive production or expenditure, for example, is readable as a symptom of the liberal ideology embedded in Keynesian or other neo-classical economics. According to this ideology, welfare production will follow from the growth of consumer production, the proper means of this having embroiled mainstream economic thought from the Enlightenment to the present. Yet from today's perspective, it is clear that the sheer extractability and mutability of things and forces undertaken in habitat production is a dimension of economic activity and wealth creation with planetary, physical limits. We churn up more of the planet (in conjunction with, one might add, more of ourselves) as so much raw material for our industrial and cultural factories. Ekins notes that such growth in biophysical throughput, or conversion of matter and energy, yields increasing entropy, hence wastes and pollution that will devalue welfare. This is uniquely the kind of growth that is not sustainable, and will lead to increasing scarcity conflicts and environmental problems if unabated. Clearly, economic welfare cannot be measured as in liberal economics, by monetary units – here in terms of domestic consumption – only. To encourage spending rather than saving, for example, as in popular Keynesianism, is a strategy that fails to register the environmental problems whose drag (both in terms of satisfaction of valued needs and desires, from a larger economics perspective, and ultimately also in monetary terms, from a conventional market perspective) will eat away at abundance rather than feed it. Another qualification to note regarding consumer production is that it comprises not only production organized by markets, but by governments or households as well; hence while monetary measurement is conventional, even when domestic economies are considered, it is an interpretive tool rather than data universally embedded in economic activity itself. Ekins notes that failing to distinguish between habitat and consumer growth in production is a central source of confusion in environmental discussion today. The positive notion of development as generalized abundance should hinge only on welfare production in some relation to consumer production, while limits to it will hinge on habitat and natural production.[9]

Returning to the problem of how modernists expressed their notions of scarcity and abundance, whether symptomatic or subversive, it is possible to distinguish between representations of abundance or excess that correlate with the production of wealth represented in consumer production, whether commercial or domestic, and those that correlate with the other three productive registers. Those expressions that correlate with consumer abundance, as a means to welfare abundance, indeed partake of the reigning liberal ideologies of their time. Yet closer examination of a variety of modernist writers and artists, including those cited as examples above, rarely sustains this correlation, because the forms of abundance we see represented in their work are hardly ever commensurate with market-valued objects and capacities, nor are the forms of scarcity commensurate with needs or desires as such. I will argue that modernists typically found the panoply of wealth produced by consumer production, no matter how beneficial or pleasing, to be essentially unsatisfying. Hence unworthy of much expenditure. On the contrary, they frequently sought to represent kinds of abundance that are neither measurable by nor yielded by consumer production, and belong rather to economic welfare and natural capital – which are achieved either directly or by way of habitat production, the mastery of biophysical throughput.

Surely Joyce, an icon of the difficult artisanal work demanded by modernist writing, confirms that an author expends labour relevant to consumer production, which, as energy and as human capital, has both physical and commodity measures in a modern economy. But just as surely, an author spends something else, a semiotic resource of emotional and meaning effects that finds its way, for example, into each, unique sentence of the wandering *Ulysses*. This resource depends not only on a stock of already manufactured semiotic production, but also on an ongoing, natural fecundity of the imagination. What is drawn from the stock of consumer production will depend in part on the literary education of the writer. This is much on display in *Ulysses*, whether canonical or pop-cultural, where its price-tags and class privilege are foregrounded in the opening two chapters. Thus the author might be seen as a semiotic reserve that accumulates or depletes itself (even goes below zero, in a sense, if plagiarizing words or rehashing ideas of others), as a result of at least two kinds of production. With respect to Joyce, it is difficult to imagine how the semiotic abundance of either the author (as a reserve) or his novel, *Ulysses* (as his expenditure, then accessible to others), could operate according to the ideas of modern market abundance, in which the degree of satisfaction must be directly proportional to a measurable accumulation or serial (iterative) consumption of meaning and affect. It is more readily believable that the notorious difficulty of modernist writing as exemplified in *Ulysses*, the extent to which its reader can cash in its language for satisfying semiotic value, diminishes rather than expands the bourgeois abundance of more conventional fiction. In the generic contracts of the latter, satisfaction is largely tied to plot and to thematization, as the marginal utility or structural outcome of emotional effects and of meaning effects, respectively. Joyce's novel scatters plot and pulverizes theme, so that value is mercurial rather than cumulative; or to put it another way, its plot and themes may be just as meaningful as in conventional fiction, but they produce a chain of modest satisfactions, rather than a revelatory experience achieved, as Eliot's Prufrock puts it, by squeezing the universe into a ball and rolling it towards a big question.[10]

Admittedly, the production of *Ulysses*, like *Mrs. Dalloway*, creates a new market object and aims to produce a new taste niche and new aesthetic desire or need. But the aesthetic achievement of either, I would suggest, is the production of a dissatisfaction with literature that merely more, and more diverse, literature will not assuage. The abundance of modern literature is already felt, indeed is the very problem. There is already an excess of ideas and sentiment circulating out there. The value of art, perhaps, is no longer to contribute originally to that circulation, to expand its conceptual or aesthetic needs and satisfactions, but rather to supplement it with needs and satisfactions not measurable by it (for example, here the pleasures of explicitly learning or acquiring semiotic processes rather than experiences or content, of reading as a vigorous and skilled labour with or without semiotic satisfaction, or of the powers and limits of the medium that carries the message). Indeed, one might argue that diverse modernisms renovated a traditional didactic value of literature in order to address the need, not for new moral or ideological content, though that too is certainly there, but for new technical skills required to sort and evaluate the abundant semiotic productivity of the new media age, literary and otherwise. Such a need cannot be met by buying and consuming what Joyce or Woolf has to say, merely, but by undertaking new acts of readerly labour to understand how

and why they say what they say, so developing skills not provided by the marketplace, effectual within and outside it. Such
a function for literature would ground it in questions of what
we need, desire, and hence value, and thus in what constitutes
abundance or scarcity most generally, opening up to critical
representation the extent to which different kinds of modern
growth are involved in our sense of well-being.

I would suggest that *Ulysses* be regarded from this perspective, less as a novelized microcosm of classical economic
exchange and its modern ideologies, than of total biophysical
throughput, both as it represents the Dublin habitat at a certain
historical moment, and as it enacts the novel as a total, entropic
product of English writing, the novel as linguistic and literary
habitat. In this view, *Ulysses* is not excessive at all, because what
it takes as its normative form is not a value measure that can be
exceeded by too much signification (like the thematic economy
of the conventional novel) but a physical measure that could
only be betrayed by inaccuracy (like a misremembered object
or an implausible thought, something *out of place*). It is con-
strained by a mimetic exercise that aims to exhaust, rather than
to unleash, its possible material, semiotic, and psychical con-
tents. So too may *Mrs. Dalloway* be comprehensible as a mimesis of throughput rather than expenditure, in which stream of
consciousness mirrors upon surfaces of individual subjectivity
– on one register a mercurial mask for the sentence itself – the
total web of physical and intangible objects and relations in yet
another modern city and day. This is not to be mistaken for a
dualism that requires Clarissa to enjoy growing flowers rather
than shopping for them. As in Joyce's work, the marketplace
and human manufacture remain genuine sources of delight.
But for all the bourgeois needs and comforts that make up the
world of this novel, both its deepest needs and satisfactions
develop elsewhere, contingent upon forms of interpersonal
recognition and emotional exchange that wander outside bourgeois circles and acknowledge the war that is the shadow side
of modern biophysical throughput, the waste in life, and the
toxicity of progress. Joyce's and Woolf's characters are heroic

not for their modern abandon to expenditure, for an unlimited seeking after new varieties of value-laden objects and capacities produced for consumption, but for the reduction of their worlds to economies of satisfaction measured by biophysical habitat conditions and welfare norms, and ultimately, perhaps unexpectedly in these gorgeous texts, for their view of economic limits. This would explain why in both novels, abundance is represented as an achievement tied to perception and interpretation, and a kind of difficult, heterodox achievement, rather than opportunity or acquisition.[11]

Of course, some modernist works, in pulling back the economic lens to this wider view, end up extending their dissatisfaction to the market and to bourgeois abundance itself, to create an explicitly oppositional ethic and aesthetic. This is the pattern of an anti-bourgeois cultural movement that expresses itself in the interrelated phenomena of aestheticism, arts and crafts, decadence and bohemianism, all inherited from the fin-de-siècle; it has as its principal worry spiritual malaise, exemplified in the arid yearnings of Eliot's *The Waste Land*. This poem anatomizes the different modes of wealth discussed above, and inverts conventional paradigms of abundance and dearth, fullness and hollowness. In so doing, it is rightly held a totem of modernist dissatisfaction and visionary scarcity, and, at the poem's obscure limits, of alternative experiences of abundance. Eliot lays out his great tableau of conventional modern wealth (in consumer production) and its ambivalent well-being in the material luxury and ennui with which the poem's second part, 'A Game of Chess,' begins. Here a woman's room is immediately the subject of the poetry, and is characterized by its load of precious materials (satin, ivory, marble, gold, gemstones) and things (throne-like chair, perfumes, artisanal décor, artworks). Yet for all her opulent surroundings, the woman expresses only an anxious boredom, concluding her dialogue with a set of despairing questions: 'What shall I do now?' and 'What shall we do tomorrow? / What shall we ever do?' In answer, the narrator of the scene thinks only of banal, routinized comforts that will suppress rather than redeem the

passage of time. Indeed, despite the wealth both of human production – industrial, artisanal, and artistic – and of life – the
speaking woman, desperate to engage with him – with which
the narrator is surrounded, he or she compares the scene to an
iconic habitat of poverty and rubbish, and of voiceless death:
'… we are in rats' alley / Where the dead men lost their bones.'
The apparent abundance is experienced as deprivation, vitality
as degraded animality or death, speech as silence. The latter
revelation conforms to the description of the woman's luxury,
whose artwork representing the Philomela myth jars the narrator, here among '… other withered stumps of time / … told
upon the walls,' 'hushing the room,' when in its own context
its truth-teller fills the ethical 'desert' of the 'sylvan scene' with
'inviolable voice.' In other words, the problem with the produced wealth of the modern setting is not simply the hollow
worth of its objects, but a kind of systemic disenchantment that
renders them ethically silent, providing no satisfying purpose
or value to either the woman or the narrator. Hence the narrator's own words, which signify narcissistically without purpose, silent in practice but overheard (so to speak) by the reader
– suspended in a pure literary act. The lower-class woman's
room in the third part of the poem, filled with things that are
more utilitarian, includes in the divan and gramophone similarly routinized and narcotic elements, similarly suppressing
an emptiness of satisfaction (and violence that can sweep into
the vacuum), as do the women's false teeth and pills, with war
in the background, later in the second part. The systemic dissatisfactions of 'A Game of Chess' echo throughout the poem,
as do its themes of inability to speak or to signify, predatory
violence, and the desertification of value. What looks like environmental abundance from a conventional economic perspective, then, reveals itself as environmental scarcity from another:
the losses of personal safety, of social belonging, of satisfying
purpose, of meaningful speech, and of durable pleasure in a
deathly, non-productive, 'waste' land.[12]

The first verses of 'A Game of Chess' allude to Shakespeare's
description of the meeting of Antony and Cleopatra on the riv-

er Cydrus, which continues to flow behind the modern scene, translated into an abundance described as overflowing its containers and drowning sense. This spectral river both evokes the water sought throughout the poem's dry landscapes, and doubles the Thames River portrayed in the subsequent part, 'The Fire Sermon.' This other tableau, at the structural centre of the poem, takes us beyond the familiar modernist critique of bourgeois wealth, taste, and ennui just discussed. We escape the room to a natural setting: the river with its littoral vegetation, and the winter landscape of dead leaves and chill wind, belong to the poem's many images of a dormant or sterile natural environment (and, of course, to the vegetation fertility myths and rituals cited in the poem's Notes). Environmental scarcity is here not merely a hollowness traversing the wealth of human productivity; it is physicalized in an infertile or inhospitable nature, both human and inhuman. The world reduced to desert-like scarcity in wealth of natural production, in fertility and regeneration, becomes the poem's most emphasized theme, foregrounded by its title, by the imagery of its opening verses and throughout, and by the head note of the Notes. Ironically, the theme is from today's 'small planet' perspective both the most prescient and the most anachronistic in the poem. It is doubtful that Eliot viewed it literally and ecologically, as an ecocritic may be tempted to do, but here, it is significant that its seasonal cycle implies the possibility of an escape from the abundance-scarcity conditions lamented in 'A Game of Chess.' This suspended possibility hangs from another thematic effect: translating his diagnosis of consumer wealth production and its regnant ideology into the language of natural wealth production creates a shock, an estrangement effect that allows us to see consumer wealth as just as totalizing and penetrating as the natural environment that we are already used to seeing as a fundamental condition of our personal, embodied life – and so to implicate both perspectives in a kind of economic crossfire of ways of understanding scarcity and abundance. Eliot asks us to hold in our minds alternative measures of satisfaction and modes of productivity, each raising questions and undoing conventional certainties of the other.

To this crossfire may be added yet a fourth perspective, which completes the fourfold typology of wealth and productivity. The river flows empty in the winter setting in which rats, bones, and the inarticulate nightingale recur. And in summer it is full of the same mundane stuff that fills the rooms in other sections of the poem. This might seem a simple repetition of the binarism of 'A Game of Chess,' but it is not. In the river, all that property is no longer stuff of value; indeed, it is no longer property. It is only the material remainder of such abundance; it is garbage. As river pollution, its imagery joins with the industrial 'oil and tar.' Abundance is viewed here as habitat throughput, as a current of material (and perhaps psychological) stuff that flows through our lives, undergoing productive or unproductive transformation. Thus Eliot's poem provides a vision not merely of modern life as a 'waste land' that is empty of satisfactions and the production of means to redeem them, but at the same time full of waste that is flotsam, ruins, detritus, and pollution, the devalued stuff that continues to flow, perhaps gushes stronger, through us as a by-product of an economic activity to which only market or market-measurable wealth is visible as a productive cause, an engine of vitality and progress. The toxicity of such by-production finds its own theme for Eliot in sexual violence, in one person taking another physically for pleasure, by force. Perhaps this is because it provides a patriarchal image of the producer (who produces in order to consume) turning his dissatisfied energies upon the conventional icon of economic consumption itself (due to her identification with the domestic realm), the woman. Into this river – not the rooms visited earlier – Eliot's narrator casts his line.

In sum, rather than providing a vision of false abundance merely from a spiritual perspective, the poem creates a series of kaleidoscopic superimpositions of human wealth creation – of productivity to satisfy needs and desires – according to diverse, even incompatible measures, which reveal the whole environment of biophysical throughput, production of goods and services, production of welfare, and production in non-human nature. For its anguished weighing of value and experience in all these registers, and the ascetic motif that emerges in result, *The Waste Land* is an exemplary expression of modernist dissatisfaction and rejection of commonplace perceptions of an abundant modernity.

Such modernisms are heterodox to their own culture of consumer abundance, and gravitate to unexpected visions of scarcity – redemptive scarcity – in their quest to redefine modern wealth, exchange, and welfare.[13] These new imaginations of both scarcity and abundance aim at the heart of the distinctively modern, twinned obsessions, on the personal scale, of leading a *full life,* and on the political scale, of a *developing* society. Such redefinitions are what the present study will attempt to survey. It should not be surprising that in so doing, the parallel problem that I introduced at the outset – the re-imagination of human in relation to animal lives – will emerge, since nonhuman creatures sharing our habitats from the dawn of time have been looked to as mediators between human wealth and welfare and the non-human environments in which these are embedded.

The first chapter will explore further the representation of biophysical throughput in relation to conventional economic production, looking at the way that avant-garde and popular artists instructively re-imagine relationships between the different kinds of wealth distinguished above. The second chapter will begin by exploring how asceticism is revived, under a program of 'making it new,' as an exercise in style, which will become the didactic or utopian register of these re-imagined economies. At the same time, style will express a new perspective upon the plasticity of human identity that turns anthropocentric common sense inside out. New kinds of characters emerge to embody such styles, figures of subjectivity that blend the human and the inhuman, that I call problem creatures. This emergence points to the profound nature of the coincidence of the phenomena of modernism in the established arts with the rise of comics as a new form – as comics is an art in which the plastic line of a graphic iconography articulates verbal language, figural language, and narrative structure alike. These modernist traditions of heterodox economic and environmental representation stretch forward to contemporary writers and artists, with both durable and changed features. The third chapter looks at how these traditions play into contemporary imaginations of time and history, and takes a closer look at scarcity itself as a historical concept. In a fourth and final chapter, I argue that the separation between iconological writing and verbal writing heretofore maintained by literature – that which until recently failed to recognize comics as literary – also conditions the suppression of children's literature more generally. Of pressing interest today is the unexpected anachronism that allows modernists to join these suppressed literary forms to speak to us across a great divide – that between a waning culture of abundance and a growing culture of scarcity – in which the modernists' attempts to embrace alternative notions of human wealth and its animal life may appear no longer prescriptive, as a cultural option, but prophetic, as a social need.

Chapter One

Modern Habitats

I have argued that *The Waste Land*, *Mrs. Dalloway*, and *Ulysses* all represent mimeses of environments of productive throughput, as a foil against which to challenge conventional notions of scarcity and abundance, and related assumptions about how value is produced and sustained in answer to needs and desires, in modern economic thinking. I have also suggested that the biophysical basis of the concept of throughput may be expanded to include materials and by-products that are not only physical (including physical energy) and biological (including labour power), as would normally be regarded by economic theorists. One might include psychical capacities and energies as well, from education skills to depression. A by-product of increased urban development and automotive technology, for example, is the quotidian affliction of road rage (yet, for the taxi driver, another by-product could be the pleasure of individual meditation or of diverse social interaction). Environmental by-products such as allergies or species migrations are biophysical, too, but not thinkable strictly as things. So, too, there is semiotic throughput: the storehouse of language and symbolic action, an intangible heritage mediated by tangible bodies and tools, which may be subject to growth and decline, development and waste. To imagine whole environments which expressed the modernity of such dimensions of economic life has been one of the fascinations of experimental artists of the past century, both in the high and low culture realms. In this chapter, I will look at the comics art of Winsor McCay, specifically his strips *Little Nemo in Slumberland* (1905–11, 1924–6; and, under the title *In the Land of Wonderful Dreams*, 1911–14) and *A Pilgrim's Progress* (1905–10); early and late writing by Gertrude Stein, *Three Lives* (1909) and *Four Saints in Three Acts* (1934); and contemporary manga art by Junko Mizuno and Takashi Murakami.

Winsor McCay is an American popular artist renowned for the idiosyncratic and gorgeous comic strips he created alternately for the *New York Herald* and for the Hearst syndicate in the early decades of the twentieth century. His most celebrated achievement, *Little Nemo*, flourished in American newspapers in the decade before the First World War, and was translated into seven languages. Like other popular comics, such as *Buster Brown*, this strip spawned numerous spin-offs in advertising and merchandise for children. It was produced as a mainstream Broadway operetta in 1908, and as an animated film in 1911 (the energetic McCay was also a film animation pioneer and vaudeville performer; he incorporated his films into his acts). The premise of the strip is both straightforward and enigmatic. Nemo is a boy (the name means 'nobody,' and alludes ambiguously to an inverted Everyman, to the wandering Odysseus, and to Jules Verne's submariner) who, in the strip's first episode, is called to Slumberland – a region somehow to be reached through the boy's own dreams – at the behest of its ruling divinity, the giant King Morpheus. In later episodes, Nemo will sometimes also seek and find guidance from another child, the Princess of Slumberland. But things always get out of hand in the world of dream and in Slumberland itself, and Nemo is nearly always chaotically diverted from his quest, and suffers a rude awakening in his bed in the last panel of each episode. The plot is strictly repetitive: in each episode the protagonist becomes increasingly lost in dream or in Slumberland proper, even while experiencing exhilaration, novelty, and adventure there, before suddenly returning to his stark bed and bare room (often to be scolded or comforted by an anxious parent). The power of the latter contrast derives from the fact that every episode begins already in dream, as if that were the normal, chronological present world; reality is only experienced as an unchanging moment of waking, as a negation.

In the first episode of *Little Nemo*, the boy is invited by a clown emissary to ride a 'night horse' to Slumberland.[1] Nemo's bedroom vanishes into the yellow colour field of his wallpaper, and as the horse begins to fly, the space turns from yellow to orange, to green, blue, red, purple, and black, while stars gradually proliferate and the panel becomes crowded with other animals riding animals in a chaotic race. Nemo is warned by the emissary, who next appears as a fantastic bird, to be good to his horse. But Nemo is careless, is pitched from his horse, and falls through black space while the stars wink out to emptiness, only to wake up on the floor beside his bed (see colour plate 3). While less narratively and verbally complex than subsequent ones, this episode establishes the economy of the strip. What is most immediately remarkable is the pointlessness of everything that appears in Nemo's dream world: nothing here answers to any discrete need or desire connected with the protagonist or plot – not the mutation of the emissary, not the changing sky colour nor its stars, not the green kangaroo ridden by a monkey nor other animals, nor the psychedelic race itself. Yet just as certainly, what is pointless is precisely what is enjoyed, both by Nemo, who readily forgets his quest in order to join this unanticipated career, and by the reader, who enjoys the fantasy of lavish colour, balletic form, and peculiar animal and human collaboration. In this mutable world of the ephemeral and unexpected into which little Nemo submerges himself, nothing answers to his desire or is valuable to him as an end. What is not anticipated cannot be desired. Everything exists bereft of narrative consequence, as a production without narrative purpose. Things can become objects of desire only at some limit of the spontaneous, at which the gap between having and not-having closes down to the blink of an eye. Yet somehow the dream world, until the rude awakening, is also one of wonderful satisfaction. If we consider the dream world as an economic environment, it is evident that everything in it expresses its contingency as throughput: Slumberland and its hinterlands are a mimesis of a total biophysical throughput in which everything is subject to production and reproduction, there is limitless energy for conversion of matter and organism, and there are no limits on abundance as such. Moreover, there is no distinction between production and by-production, between production for consumable or useful ends, and waste: such a distinction is meaningless, where all is waste and yet all is valuable. This world is akin to the primitivist one in which all human activity blends into the harmony of an idealized, abundant nature. Indeed, here too within this world, we find no distinction between manufactured consumer production and natural fertility.

To the extent that McCay's Slumberland expresses an allegory of desire, it fails to produce its plotted object, which is the closure of a meeting with Morpheus that would symbolize Nemo's arrival at a position of mastery in the world of dream. Nor does the Beatrice figure of the Princess, borrowed from Dante, offer adequate guidance to this end. Of course, neither psychoanalytically, nor formally (as an episodic narrative), can this be surprising. She functions only, like everything else emanating from Slumberland, to sustain the dream, to keep it going for Nemo, or to keep him going as a dream figure himself. (Her opposite number is the trickster Flip, a kind of abject demi-god from the liminal world of Dawn.) The magic of this endlessly unsatisfied allegory, then, is the ease with which such mastery of desire, which is as much as to say a mastery over the production of one's entire environmental world, is superseded by the quotidian bliss of limitless abundance, not of things manufactured to answer to one's need or desire, but of purely aesthetic wonders – the unanticipated delights of a brave new world – generated by a post-human throughput of human, animal, and inorganic mutation. It is not that the dream is always happy; it may inspire fear, but never longing. Here, one does not need to need, nor desire to desire, except (and significantly) holistically, in order to continue dreaming: to sustain the total environment, or if that is too much, one's footing in it, including one's dream kin – the Princess, Flip, Impy, and others of whom Nemo both takes care and seeks help. McCay's fantasy verges on an ecological one, in which what we desire is reconstructed and reduced to a principle of holistic conservation and ephemeral property, in a world envisioned economically as a post-human throughput of habitat wealth, which we cannot master.

Hence in *Little Nemo* the endless alternation of proliferation, mutation, and elimination of things, creatures, spaces, and even its own cartoon lines and panels. Hence, too, its shadow side in McCay's concurrent strip, *A Pilgrim's Progress*. In this strip, the dream world of abundance disappears, and we find ourselves in an empty desert setting of blank panel space bisected by a flat horizon line, relieved by occasional outcroppings of rock. It is the world of Eliot's waste land, of barren aridity without shelter, deprived of the water of life, lacking place for roots, human or otherwise, to fasten and grow. McCay's wanderer in this landscape is a black-suited bourgeois man in frock coat and top hat, whose only desire is to rid himself of the valise he carries marked DULL CARE. In one episode, afflicted with 'awful monotony,' he encounters a goat he supposes to feel vital and happy. The goat charges his valise, raising the man's hopes of its destruction, but the valise is unexpectedly stronger, and the blow kills the animal. In another episode, a man promises to send his friend RELIEF, but after waiting Godot-like on the same rocks for the remainder of the episode, while growing from youth to age, the man with DULL CARE gives up and moves on.[2] This is the world that Slumberland escapes: the world of endless dissatisfaction, of allegorical scarcity – allegorical, because the clothes of the man index his worldly success, his access to wealth of the marketplace and social relations of his time. His daily inability to exchange, convert, or destroy the luggage of his *ennuyant* possessions (whatever is within the valise) is as darkly comical in repetition as Nemo's nightly freedom from them.

This contrast is captured in the framework of *Little Nemo* itself, in which the waste land of dull care has its extension in the boy's austere bed and barren bedroom, the only visitors

to which are his tiresomely unimaginative elders, who act as
disciplinary emissaries, whether comforting or aggressive, of a
colourless world beyond. From a waking perspective, Nemo's
night world is pure waste, even a kind of pollution: unproductive experience that merely gets in the way of rest, the recov-
ery of energy, for whatever must be done the coming day. In
other words, the economic imagination of the strip turns on a
central irony. It imagines a utopian abundance alternative to
the dystopian scarcity of modern bourgeois life, by switching
its perspective of desire and productivity from a conventionally modern capacity or object-satisfaction world of consumer wealth to an environmental throughput world of habitat
wealth. Yet this very imagination is portrayed as the fantasy
by-product of the latter reality, a kind of parasitical growth.
This irony plays itself out in the way that the alternative economic imagination, with its structure of feeling subversive to
conventional constructions of desire and need, and to ideas of
scarcity and abundance, is recontained in the commodity form
of the periodical newspaper itself. The comic strip is sold and
bought; it is not even – like books or even like newspapers later
in the century – normally held by public libraries, though it may
be shared among family members or friends. As a newsprint
commodity, its principal function was to provide eye-catching
entertainment that would help sell the news, including to less
literate readers, in a highly competitive American journalism
industry. As the name 'comics' reveals, this popular art form
was also intended to be mainly humorous – though adventure
comics also grew popular in the decades after the War. In any
case, comics were judged by their executive producers for their
escapist or therapeutic value – for laughs and sensation, not
disquiet or subversion. McCay's strips were more aestheticized
than most, but participated in the same economy of newspaper .
advertising and consumable pleasure. If one can briefly live
Nemo's dream with Nemo, and return to it every week, it may
help to assuage the dull cares of the other, real world.

It might be difficult at first to imagine a correlative of McCay's
comics art in literary writing. What kind of art of the printed

word will allow the narrative and semiotic flow of language to draw us into an environment of its own, where there is no sensual colour and form to seduce the eye, no human, animal, or other gaze to hail the I, but only its own unlimited production of sufficient meaning? What could a mimesis of environmental throughput, or habitat wealth, look like in merely verbal writing? I have already suggested that we can see this mimesis as one dimension of a variety of modernist texts, but only in Gertrude Stein's work, so far as I know, is it developed as an end in itself.

For Stein, as she explains in *Lectures in America* (1935), plots are uninteresting, insofar as narrative desire will always cancel out immediate verbal expression in the service of a narrative production that recalls an abstraction of the past (previous plot gleaned from words) in the service of an abstraction of the future (desired plot closure). Who cares who succeeds or fails in their story? She is tired of successes and failures, the conventional production of narrative desire that she finds emptily repetitive. But modernity has provided her, in its newspapers and certain pulp genres, indeed in comics or 'funny papers' itself, an alternative aesthetic, one free of bad repetition and hence authentically abundant in literary expression, worthy of literary desire: 'In all these [new popular genres] it is the moment to moment emphasis in what is happening that is interesting, the succeeding and failing is really not the thing that is interesting.' Stein is here defending the allegedly repetitive nature of her writing, so that 'moment to moment emphasis' refers to the serial occurrence not simply of narrative content but of words themselves. There is an ontological as well as a literary side to this, because her interest in serial, 'moment to moment' syntax, sentence, and narrative structures responds to her existentialist perception that 'it is never the same moment it is never the same emphasis at any successive moment of existing.' Writing must, like cinematic frames, combine its differential elements holistically, producing an ongoing perception of compositional production itself; otherwise, it will sacrifice its immediate expression to abstractions of memory mixed with desire, to a sterile recognition of anticipated meanings. The only thing that does not change, which is absolute, is the individual uniqueness of productive agency in one's environment, an individual talent who works in and on the social, sensual, and verbal 'composition we live in.'[3]

This idea of writing is developed as a practice as early as *Three Lives*, in which narrative gives way to the episodic in what sometimes seems nothing more than a string of anecdotes telling the lives of three modern, working-class women. In each, we are inevitably hooked by the narrative desire to know, what will finally happen to her? In each, the answer is simply, what *is* happening to her. In the first story about a housekeeper, 'The Good Anna,' there is never a clear distinction between what has narrative value and what is merely a colourful aside. Consider the following anecdote:

> Out of the whole collection of stray creatures, it was the young Peter and the jolly little Rags, Anna could not find it in her heart to part with. These became part of the household of the good Anna's Miss Mathilda.
>
> Peter was a very useless creature, a foolish, silly, cherished, coward male. It was wild to see him rush up and down in the back yard, barking and bouncing at the wall, when there was some dog out beyond, but when the very littlest one there was got inside of the fence and only looked at Peter, Peter would retire to his Anna and blot himself out between her skirts.
>
> When Peter was left downstairs alone, he howled. 'I am all alone,' he wailed, and then the good Anna would have to come and fetch him up. Once when Anna stayed a few nights in a house not far away, she had to carry Peter all the way, for Peter was afraid when he found himself on the street outside his house. Peter was a good sized creature and he sat there and he howled, and the good Anna carried him all the way in her own arms. He was a coward was this Peter, but he had kindly, gentle eyes and pretty collie head, and his fur was very thick and white and nice when he was washed. And then Peter never strayed away, and he looked out of his nice eyes and he liked it when you rubbed him

down, and he forgot you when you went away, and he barked whenever there was any noise.[4]

The point of all this, from a conventional plot perspective, is to provide yet another example of the altruism of the 'good Anna,' who devotes her life to taking care of others, often at her own expense. Yet Peter, rather than Anna, is insistently the grammatical subject of these paragraphs, in which Anna remains a background figure. If the point were to establish Anna's character, or even to establish an authoritative realism as its medium, we would require neither this foregrounding of Peter as narrative agency and object, nor the many details that defy necessity (he can be a realist dog merely as a generic dog, rather than taking on an individual identity of his own) and, in the final sentence, dwindle into a haphazard list. No, Peter is decidedly to be consumed by the reader, 'for himself,' both as narrative content, as a spontaneously animated, unexpected character akin to McCay's dream creatures, and in sheer form, as a pleasurable experience of Stein's writing style.

Nothing goes to waste in this style: nothing is set aside or shucked off as insignificant by-product in deference to the production of narrative function and ends. In the crucible of this style, narrative is broken down into the seriality of what happens, now belonging to the mimesis of a total through-put of story elements, in which the meaning to be gleaned (or 'Anna') is inseparable from a shifting realist environment and verbal composition. This mode of storytelling, considered as a type of economic production, defies the conventional need or desire to hear 'stories about' (the success or failure of ...) and their comparative satisfactions. Rather, such storytelling tries to register its subject matter as a total composition in process, one in which satisfaction, dissatisfaction, and indifference – or meaning, enigma, and insignificance – are interdependent, equally inconsequential, and equally to be accounted for. From one perspective, as in *Little Nemo*, the story has no discernible meaning: semiotically, it is all by-product or waste. Thus we find Stein boring, merely repetitive. Yet from another perspective, also similarly, all is valuable. What counts in a story are its by-products and waste, so that its subject matter is always embedded in – and so its truth is somehow to be measured by – the unexpected, unuseful consumption of an unaccountable narrative development and authorial style.

This stylistic crucible reaches its realist narrative limit in Stein's last-completed of the three lives, 'Melanctha.' Here, not only is narrative and its conventional emplotment of desire broken down into an environment of throughput, but the process extends to the very 'moment to moment' composition of the event and the sentence. Here are the thoughts of Jeff Campbell lying on the grass with Melanctha:

> Jeff never, even now, knew what it was that moved him. He never, even now, was ever sure, he really knew what Melanctha was, when she was real herself, and honest. He thought he knew, and then there came to him some moment, just like this one, when she really woke him up to be strong in him. Then he really knew he could know nothing. He knew then, he never could know what it was she really wanted with him. He knew then he never could know really what it was he felt inside him. It was all so mixed up inside him. All he knew was he wanted very badly Melanctha should be there beside him, and he wanted very badly, too, always to throw her from him. What was it really that Melanctha wanted with him? What was it really, he, Jeff Campbell, wanted she should give him? 'I certainly did think now,' Jeff Campbell groaned inside him, 'I certainly did think now I really was knowing all right, what I wanted. I certainly did really think now I was knowing how to be trusting with Melanctha. I certainly did think it was like that now with me sure, after all I've been through all this time with her. And now I certainly do know I don't know anything that's very real about her. Oh the good Lord help and keep me!' and Jeff groaned hard inside him, and he buried his face deep in the green grass underneath him, and Melanctha Herbert was very silent there beside him.[5]

By the time the reader reaches the penultimate sentence, 'And now I certainly do know I don't know anything that's very real about her,' she or he has stumbled over the intricate rubble of what Jeff may know and what may be real (twelve verbal instances of the first, ten of the second), has seen each of these concepts and others turned incrementally in usage or context to different meanings associated with the same subject, as each sentence takes off in endless fractal growth from the last, each folded back on the other by a 'then,' a 'now,' and by gerunds floating in time. The reader is finally less expectant of a centre or resolution to these mundane yet subtle, multiple realities and knowledges – that is, even at the level of progress through a single sentence – than he or she becomes fascinated by Stein's emotional, intellectual, and linguistic factory chugging away, pouring a hundred things into the story environment among which one seeks in vain for the intended product, some sign that can be exchanged for knowledge of who Jeff really is, and what's really going on here. Stein produces the mimesis of a lived moment in which barely complete or contradictory, unproductive words and thoughts are as valuable to charac-ter and event as those ultimately resolved or articulated. This emotional and psychological noise, and its waste land of verbal permutation which seems at first to obscure what the character really thinks and what will develop the plot, becomes itself the object of interest, and an unexpected satisfaction.

By the time of *Four Saints in Three Acts*, this style has shed even its psychological realism and become a purely verbal environment – still meaningful, of course, but as a landscape of story and character fragments held together by the sheer experience of a writing style, propelled by a concrete poetry of sound: 'How many saints can be and land be and sand be and on a high plateau there is no sand there is snow and there is made to be so and very much can be what there is to see when there is a wind to have it dry and be what they can understand to undertake to let it be to send it well as much as none to be to be behind. None to be behind. Enclosure.' As this quotation suggests, the opera's concerns are not evidently transcenden-tal, and rather evoke inhabiting an arid land and constructing a place to live there as a saint, to find abundance amid scarcity. What a saint means to Stein is suggested by the dominant figure of her composition, Saint Teresa of Avila, who is remembered for her mystical writings in the genre of spiritual exercises, and for her founding of convents and monasteries with a renewed zeal for poverty. Renouncing social and financial wealth, Saint Teresa found in asceticism – the word derives from the Greek for 'exercises,' and affiliates a rejection of socially valued abundance with writing and revelatory imagination – a new kind of satisfaction, and the possibility of communities built around it. Such communities are at once enclosures (appropriating a waste territory, a devalued landscape, at the cost of rejecting the stuff and desires of an unsanctified life) and liberations (to a new permeability of signs and things, and new measures of growth): 'Some and sum. Add sum. Add some. / Let it in around. / With seas. / With knees. / With keys. / With pleases. / Go and know. / In clouded. / Included. / Saint Therese and attachment. With any one please. / No one to be behind and enclosure. Suddenly two see. / Two and ten. / Saint Two and Saint Ten.'[6] Stein's style becomes a spiritual exercise for the modern secular imagination, an ascetic renunciation and reconstruction of the feelings of desire and satisfaction through an experience of language as economic throughput. This aestheticization of an alternative economic order, as a sensual and verbal asceticism, is prefigured long ago in *Three Lives*, in which all the working-class women are ascetic in this sense. The good Anna, Melanctha, and the gentle Lena are all indifferent to worldly gain; they reject the pursuit of conventional abundance in devotion to obscure mysteries, respectively, of care, wisdom, and peace.

The idealism of Stein's economic vision is nicely summed up in *Lectures in America*: 'If you write the way it has already been written the way writing has already been written then you are serving mammon, because you are living by something some one has already been earning or has earned. If you write as you are to be writing then you are serving as a writer god because you are not earning anything.'[7] Bad repetition, which is (reproducing) writing for a product, to satisfy conventional narrative desire, is to sacrifice writing to earning. Good repetition, which is the total throughput of 'writing as you are,' earns nothing – is both waste, and paradoxically, in this assimilation to Christian allegory, the only measure of worth. But a reader may be forgiven for remaining skeptical before this literary transcendence of mammon. Was not Stein's rentier lifestyle, which allowed her to live comfortably without employment – and to have household servants, travel, collect art, and subsidize her own small-press publications – rather complacently dependent on the business wealth of her family? Neither consumer marketplace wealth nor a literary engagement in it troubled her. Though she was able initially to publish many of her literary works only in little magazines and small art presses, her first ambition was always trade publication and slick magazines. This was not so that she could make more money, but so that she could be more widely read. She actively sought to have her work commodified in a commercial print marketplace, even as her work subverted the measures of commodity desire and satisfaction. This was not a contradiction for Stein because her alternative economy was individualist and epistemological in motivation, not altruistic or political: to have one's economic sensibilities dislocated through immersion in what may be called a literature of throughput is to join her, like Saint Theresa, in a new cultural enclave, but in the same modern landscape. Renounce the modern machinery of desire and abundance, but depend on it, as that of which you are the unintended and unvalued, hence liberated, by-product. 'There has been an incredible reason for their planning,' says Saint Chavez of Saint Theresa's community, 'what is not by any manner of means their allowance in having let it be theirs by negligence.' Modernism may serve god rather than mammon, but mammon, for the same unexpected reason, may still serve modernism.[8]

The dialectic of subversion and recontainment of economic ideology – of the very feelings we have about what we need and lack, and what kind of environment seems to us either plentiful or barren – that is played out in the art of Gertrude

Stein and Winsor McCay may be found elsewhere in the art of their generation and beyond. The dialectic has achieved an astonishing explicitness in certain manga art of today. Junko Mizuno's graphic novel *Pure Trance* (1998) imagines a future world in which the planet has been ravaged by biological warfare, and surviving human life has enclosed itself in a manufactured, sanitized underground environment. It is a dystopia of consumption: the only food source is a nutrient liquid called Pure Trance, a single artificial substance that appears in myriad product forms, simulating diversity. The women of the Overeaters Treatment Centre, where most of the story is set, consume it in any form, indiscriminately and excessively, even intravenously like a drug, as if paradoxically, endlessly unsatisfied by the utopian abundance of Pure Trance. This pathology is normal in Mizuno's Foucauldian dystopia, where the sadistic OTC Director is the society's most powerful authority, rather than the vacuous head of state.

The story is vague and episodic, and as in McCay's and Stein's work, the biophysical and semiotic landscapes of false abundance, of repressed hunger or scarcity, and of an alternative economy of desire and need, are what fascinate. The latter offers a curious twist on the primitivist fantasy of natural wealth: the heroine escapes the OTC onto the post-human planet above ground, hunts and forages to survive, and achieves a new experience of abundance – not in any simpler, idealized Nature, however, but in a mutated, complex, surreal environment in which she must first conquer her fear of and accept a disintegration of human-animal-plant distinctions in a brave new world of fertile, genetic chaos (see fig. 1.1). Also akin to McCay's and Stein's work, Mizuno's comics paradoxically embrace their commodity form: this graphic novel was originally published serially as a bonus insert for a CD series by a mainstream music distributor (1996–8) – functioning very much as Golden Age comics did, to sell a host product – before being rewritten for book publication by a manga publisher. Mizuno has maintained this association between comics art and commodity manufacturing, in designing vinyl

1.1 Junko Mizuno, *Pure Trance* (1998), English edition (San Francisco: Last Gasp, 2005), p. 158. © 2005 Mizuno Junko.

dolls, stuffed animals, stationery, comics, and clothing merchandise all vertically tied in with manga-derived art that has broken into the high art market. What distinguishes her work from McCay and Stein, however, is the serene postmodernism with which its aesthetic form and content already embody the commodity world which mediates it. The figures of people, creatures, and plant life which fill *Pure Trance* are in the *kawaii* or cute tradition of Japanese mass culture, inflected by a sado-cute or horror-cute of underground manga style. The style is reminiscent of Hello Kitty, Pokemon, My Little Pony, and other child merchandise brands, but with a twist: imagine the Care Bears in a Frida Kahlo painting or a Hugh Hefner magazine. Cute is never ironized or undercut: it is simply ubiquitous.

This totality of cute is no mere aesthetic matter. Mizuno has said that in *Pure Trance* she wanted nostalgically to create a world out of Hello Kitty and other doll and toy brands of her childhood: its figures are already icons of commodities.[9] This iconicity is reinforced in the real world by Mizuno's series of horror-cute stuffed dolls and plastic figurines, similar to the creatures in *Pure Trance*, available as 'collectibles' in the youth and toy market. Thus, in a modernist gesture of her own, the writer draws a utopian distinction between god and mammon, between the commodity consumption dystopia of Pure Trance and the brave new fertility of a post-human planet. But with the brash non-irony of a postmodernist, she refuses the necessity of this distinction in art (fashion, toy) production, serving both god and mammon, refusing to build the enclosure of a difficult style or of a dream from which we must awake. She will celebrate mammon, modern consumer wealth and production, for providing the very sign system and emotional palette required to render an alternative economic vision, of habitat production and natural production, both legible and, yes, satisfying to all comers.

Is such artistic production subversive or complacent? A shock to the system, or a sellout? I would call it a kind of commodity asceticism, in which (1) commodity production and consumption is revealed to be embedded in an environment of biophysical by-products and waste (the post-human risks of the planet surface; or the compulsions/addictions of sadism, overeating, and illicit meat-eating in the enclosed city, which express a chronically dissatisfied, nihilist violence against self or others); and (2) market choice, the appropriation of select commodities (the market niche of something like a Mizuno brand), is re-imagined as a kind of renunciation, not transcendental or elitist but popular and materialist, horizontal if you like, a re-imagining of mere taste as a spiritual exercise that finds value only in market production having the structure of feeling for habitat and natural production. At its best, such commodity asceticism might freshly illuminate and challenge a humanist and anthropocentric economic ideology, whose faith in commodity abundance as the key to human satisfaction has manufactured the personal neuroses, social pathologies, and peculiar violence of the modern age, and whose drive to master an externalized Nature has brought the planet within sight of catastrophe. At worst, such commodity asceticism might complacently reproduce only an escapist experience of subversive knowledge and transfigured desire, leaving all but the consumer in the act of consuming the ultimately, satisfactorily cute, to their fate.

Such ambiguity is, infamously, the explicit basis of another manga-based artist's career: Takashi Murakami creates iconic figures that he reproduces in a vast variety of media and merchandise, cutting across high art and commercial enterprise, from acrylic canvases to fashion accessories to monumental sculptures to plastic toys, conflating artist and brand, gallery and store. His Kaikai Kiki Co., Ltd., has branch offices in Tokyo and New York in whose dizzying vertical structure products are designed and fabricated, intellectual property rights negotiated and lent, and the business of brands, advertising, exhibitions, lectures, and critical commentary, manufacturing out-sourcing, importing and exporting, and much else undertaken with industrial zeal. He has successfully troubled, as Scott Rothkopf has observed, not only the modernist divide between art and mass culture, between work of art and commercial merchandise, but also between modern individual and corporate identity.[10] Murakami's work is emphatically marked by the mimesis of biophysical throughput that is narrativized in *Pure Trance*, but it is here broken down into a scattered, fragmentary, fitfully serialized world of production itself (at once the vehicle of his work and its content) reminiscent of Stein's verbal art. Also similar to Mizuno, Murakami pushes a ubiquity of cute to unsettling horizons, and generates icons of consumption embedded in biophysical violence (his hyper-eroticized waitress figure, named *Hiropon* or 'crystal meth' [1997]; his self-portrait as a bulimic cartoon vomiting his own cartoon products in the painting *Tan Tan Bo Puking* [2002]; or the transfiguration of the atomic mushroom cloud into a cute icon in his *Time Bokan* series). Moreover, this iconology is similarly and ecstatically entangled in post-human fertility (the materialist, genetic abandon of his monumental Buddha-like sculpture series; the monstrous permutations of his Mickey Mouse–like cartoon character, DOB). Murakami's work produces in commodities, specifically commodities associated with his corporate identity, the utopian mimesis of an unlimited environment, an indiscriminate, by-productive, ambivalently cute-ecstatic-abject abundance liberated from the pursuit of a conventional, self-affirming, merely comforting abundance of fulfilled needs and desires.

It is perhaps difficult to imagine a literary correlative of Murakami today, in which Stein's modernist economies are programmatically reabsorbed into demotic, mass culture realms, her avant-garde verbal hieroglyphs into popular consumer scripts. It is tempting to see these economies find their ultimate, hieratic form in the writing of Jacques Derrida, which is about writing itself taken to be the ineradicable trace of the repressed, unproductive, material waste by-production of language, where language is supposed properly to be consumed into meaning (and metaphysics!) – a toxic economy of meaning-production in which Derrida's own writing participates in order performatively to enact its inherited logical and ideological costs, sacrifices, by-production, and waste. Preparing the English-language reader for his own writing, Derrida cautions that while such writing may seem unproductive, yet it inscribes 'the impossibility of reducing a text as such to its effects of meaning, content, thesis, or theme' – or rather – Derrida here performatively changes his words mid-sentence, inserts a Flaubertian cliché, and invents a word, enacting language as expressive throughput – 'not the impossibility, perhaps, since *it is commonly done*, but the resistance – we shall call it the *restance*,' a neologism Barbara Johnson translates as 'the fact or act of remaining or of being left over.'[11] Yet a comparable art of the printed word in English, one that would like *Pure Trance* overtly appropriate commodity form and desire in order to express a strange new asceticism, is not easy to imagine. There is the new genre of the blog, in which we confront the banality of dissemination, in writing as fiction/non-fiction, truth/untruth, valuable/waste production – the sheer pleasure of writing (and writerly reading), which Roland Barthes did not live to see realized for its own sake in mundane proliferation – and must pay our electronic equipment and service provider to do so. But it is a symptom of the society of the spectacle, a modernity that brings graphically and colourfully to life whole fantasy environments for identification and consumption associated with brands – the 'commercial utopias,' says Naomi Klein, of a global 'branded village' – that the comics world of iconography will register this fault line in modern economic structures of feeling more readily than the written word.[12]

But this distinction, too, Takashi Murakami has troubled. The most represented figure in his oeuvre, a Mickey Mouse–like cartoon figure called Mr. DOB, is a curiously verbal icon, having the letters *D* and *B* written on his round ears and an *O* around his face. A kind of verbal icon performing a verbal icon, he represents 'an inquiry,' writes Murakami, 'into the 'secret of market survival,' or the 'universality' of characters like Mickey Mouse, Sonic the Hedgehog, Doraemon, Miffy, Hello Kitty, even the Hong Kong–made rip-offs.'[13] DOB is a constantly changing, ambiguous creature, however, that defies identification with a single meaning, purpose, or affect, and is frequently embedded in environments of post-human creaturely life or expressionistic media from which it is impossible (or since it is surely commonly done, is it rather *restance*?) to glean a stable or satisfying iconic recognition. The name or logo DOB is an absurdist neologism, derived from a manga reference to a mispronunciation of the word 'why' compounded with a sexual pun to yield a dada-like incantation, *dobojite dobojite oshamanbe*, abbreviated to a logo. Yet this postmodern subversion of desire belongs to a program of ascetic rather than agitprop exercises, its utopia not a communal appropriation of the wealth of marketplace production, the program of the left, but rather an aesthetic revelation of marketplace production in its larger economic environment, to be enjoyed, however ambiguously, by a radical liberalism. In the Poundian vortex of DOB, the detours of desire through the dark materials of their own culture industry must also recognize the commodity as the classical icon of individual capital and innovation: 'The concept of originality is the lifeline of contemporary art and culture as a whole,' Murakami has said, defending a legal claim against the producer of a DOB look-alike: 'I consider the respect for intellectual property as an essential element for the development of ideas and culture in our societies.'[14] Thus Murakami's corporate identity is both akin to Disney (which has notoriously pursued legal action against copies and parodies of Mickey Mouse) and, in infusing the commodity with a kind of aesthetic transparency to its productive world in biophysical labour and nature, is in its edgy expressive notion of self (satisfaction), utterly different.

Writing is fully appropriated to this postmodern program in Murakami's work with the Louis Vuitton fashion accessory brand. Collaborating with the Moët Hennessy Louis Vuitton corporation, Murakami designed two series of handbags: 'Eye Love Monogram' intersperses colourful LV brand monograms, and the stylized japoniste lotuses that are the Vuitton logo, with Murakami's jellyfish eyes – figures drawn from his paintings that appear in this context as Murakami's collaborative branding of the merchandise (he retains ownership of the design); and 'Cerises' overprints the LV monogram with

Murakami's cute cherries. While the latter series plays on the consumption of the brand name, LV, the former gazes back at the consumer with the genetic chaos of Mr. DOB, while punning with gleeful Derridean impertinence on I/eye and love/ LV. These designs are not confined to LVMH merchandise, but become major acrylic-on-canvas paintings. The 'Eye Love Monogram' design is enlarged and refined for the 1.8 metre square *Eye Love SUPERFLAT* diptych (2003–4), while in the vast 3.5 metre square *The World of Sphere* (2003), the 'Eye Love Monogram' divides and coalesces into swirling cloud or amoeba figures, from which a horror-cute panda on a bamboo-studded crag and another floating creature peer out, in a weird-cute, postmodern version of a classical East Asian landscape of the spiritual pilgrimage genre (see colour plates 4 and 5). Writing here fuses the calligraphy of classical art with the monogram of commercial branding, and seems to belong to an economy in which the human and its other – in nature, in commerce, in writing – are ecstatically deconstructed.

In this chapter, I have argued that a tradition in modernist and postmodernist writing has challenged commonly held views of economic abundance and satisfaction proper to the modern age, by re-imagining economic life as a biophysical *habitat* continually transformed by at least four incommensurable types of wealth production and their repressed experiences of scarcity.

For the modernists, this re-imagination of our economic habitat was a reaction to feelings of hollowness or violence within modern abundance, and led to the re-invention of *style* as the vehicle of an avant-garde *asceticism*. Modernist asceticism, appropriating to secular conditions the spiritual exercises of renunciation and devotion of a religious genre, expresses itself in practices of self-exile, the renunciation of dominant measures of wealth, and praise of alternative experiences of productivity and satisfaction, encoded in the form and content of an experimental literary art. Yet these new visions of economic life and ascetic reaction may seem, in hindsight, somewhat idealistic or abstract: they were not contingent upon the biophysical limits to abundance that a *fin-de-millénaire* perception of a small planet has since imposed. Postmodernists such as Junko Mizuno and Takashi Murakami are aware of this ecological contingency, and respond with boldly aestheticized representations of sustainable development: in their work, commodity economies insistently provide the very language of value and legibility, and arguably the driving force as well, whereby a new kind of wealth and satisfaction may be recognized; and they do so not by repressing alternative economies in our habitat, but imbued with tenacious postmodern optimism even in the face of ecological holocaust (for example, the cute, cheerful flowers sprouting from the eyes of the mushroom cloud in Murakami's *Time Bokan* series, or the biological warfare that ravages the planet in Mizuno's *Pure Trance* and leads to new, human/non-human hybrids), they drag the structures of feeling demanded by our heretofore repressed *supplements* in post-human nature and technology up into the iconological experience – the contingent *logos* – of the commodity itself. Thus we are asked to experience the satisfaction of a commodity not as object or service, but as vortex and habitat. Both Mizuno's and Murakami's work celebrates harmonious and sympathetic relations between creaturely lives in the face of a needlessly violent, oppressive modernity rooted in the commodity as fetish, and they offer the commodity as a habitat that defies anthropocentric mastery, as a solution.

Chapter Two

Problem Creatures

Though economic visions are diverse in modernist and post-modernist art, it will be evident from the preceding discussions that the renunciation of conventional abundance, the radical questioning of needs and desires, and the search for alternative forms of wealth and satisfaction seem to have a common iconology with which the reader is invited to identify: the creaturely synthesis of human and animal, sometimes human and technological (including the technology of writing), sometimes all three. This post-human figure ranges across hybrid species, from the simian Sweeney to Slumberland's strange denizens, to the lexically dislocated animals and saints that supplement *Three Lives* and *Four Saints in Three Acts*, to the myriad life forms invented in global comics and manga since McCay's day. To fully retrace the long genealogy of this icon in the modern age is more than this study can attempt. Its most common manifestation, the synthesized animal-human figure, is the subject of the following pages. Because it is a speculative creature, studying it will not tell us anything more about non-human animals 'in themselves,' but only in their historical or imagined syntheses with human life and subjectivity, and, in particular, insofar as their otherness from yet codependency with human life leaves its traces – gazes back from the faces, or hails us in the voices, of modernist style. Modernist and subsequent experimental writers have imaginatively birthed generation after generation of post-human creatures who are the protagonists of an alternative economic experience and, instructively, of a dystopian, or more often utopian, future for our erstwhile human history.[1]

It will be helpful, before examining such creatures and their experimental habitats in this didactic light, to place the modern ideology of abundance and scarcity discussed in the Introduction in a wider historical and aesthetic perspective. Although the period stretching from before the Great War through the Jazz Age and into the Thirties is marked by great contrasts of material excess and dearth, and by changes in duties to work, save, or spend, the period may also be situated in a longer economic modernity whose overarching ideology, with respect to scarcity and abundance, has been influentially narrated by political scientist Nicholas Xenos. Xenos begins with the proposition that scarcity and abundance are socially and historically defined concepts rather than natural or scientific constants, and are thus in the terrain of ideology. He argues that from the eighteenth century forward, the modern age has been generally unable to feel or think of needs as clearly distinct from desires: what may one day seem a luxury, may the next day seem a necessity; what now feels like a necessity, may tomorrow be an anachronism. Standards of food, shelter, and clothing – or, likewise, of mental and physical health – are not given by raw nature, but by habit, adaptation, imagination, and desire in relation to a particular functioning society. Enlightenment writers David Hume and Adam Smith considered the modern proliferation of marketplace products and services, and the newly defined needs and desires embodied in them, to express the very essence of civilized progress – a universal, ever-increasing refinement of taste and enjoyment of human capacities and satisfactions. Scarcity in this view is no longer felt to be the result of a natural event, such as seasonal drought or disease, but as a permanent, generalized condition of modern society. And one to be embraced! For this generalized scarcity is the engine of a generalized abundance, of an ever-flourishing wealth. The modern person is a restless thing, always pursuing new desires, admitting new dependencies, and, in a terrible sense, never satisfied. Yet he or she is in another sense always flowering, discovering new feelings, experiences, and satisfactions – unveiling the unlimited complexity of the soul.

Of course, this is the economic vision of a consumer, and while all moderns are consumers, only those with considerable capital have the consumer power to feel and to realize the ideal refinements of this economic ideology. It cannot yet be an ideology of the lower classes, and indeed, as Xenos observes, what was once thought naturally to exist as a degree or caste in society, however to be pitied or improved, became in the labouring class, a more intimate and ambivalent rebuke: 'The great advances in commerce and industry that were so palpably a legacy of the eighteenth century, and which would become the obsession of the nineteenth, were inextricably bound up with the creation of a universe of desire. Yet the labouring poor were an unmistakable by-product of those advances, and they loomed as unintegrated threats to that universe.'[2] The drive to integrate all classes, functionally if not equally, into the structure of feeling of such a universe – to liberate them into a generalized scarcity that will be created and mastered by an expanding, productive, industrial modernity they may claim as their own – is common to diverse political economic movements, Left and Right, from then to now. This political drive, whose earliest icon is Marx, has often influentially if ambivalently been fused with another quite different one, whose whistle-blower was Rousseau: a subjective reaction against the false promise of this modern economic ideology *tout court*, and an effort to refashion it within alternative views of scarcity and wealth.

Xenos sees the latter tradition as a type of Romantic radicalism that stalks the lonely margins of modern economic thought. While not significant as a determining force in political history, this tradition does provide a heritage for the heterodox economies I have discussed in modernist and postmodernist literature and iconic arts. It is a tradition somewhat eccentric to that of modern class struggle, which has warred over property production (signally, over private versus collective property structures) as the key to welfare production, and has until recent decades largely ignored or sidelined the biophysical dimension of habitat production and its interdependencies with conditions of natural fertility and biodiversity. 'Unlike their progressivist contemporaries, J.S. Mill and Karl Marx,' the Romantic radical tradition of Thomas Carlyle, John Ruskin, and William Morris, following Rousseau, drew on shocking, exotic, or anachronistic images or styles in order to 'alter the metaphors through which society and history were understood, and in so doing to alter the actions of men and women, resulting in a fundamentally transformed society in which abundance would be realized immediately.' These writers wished nothing less than to reform human desire, in exemplary form through writing itself, so as to transfigure commonplace notions of what it means to be human. They took habitat and natural production to be sufficient – a realm of biophysical plenty ready to sustain the welfare of all, materially, sensually, and socially – but a realm that was all but eclipsed by the shadow of property production, in which desire is truncated by the poverty created by class difference, and hollowed out by the ennui of generalized scarcity. 'England is full of wealth, of multifarious produce, supply for human want in every kind,' says Carlyle, 'yet England is dying of inanition':

> With unabated bounty the land of England blooms and grows; waving with yellow harvests; thick-studded with workshops, industrial implements, with fifteen millions of workers, understood to be the strongest, the cunningest and the willingest our Earth ever had; these men are here; the work they have done, the fruit they have realized is here, abundant, exuberant on every hand of us: and behold, some baleful fiat as of Enchantment has gone forth, saying, 'Touch it not, ye workers, ye master-idlers, none of you can touch it, no man of you shall be the better for it; this is enchanted fruit!'[3]

Where abundance is measured not only by the property capital of market measures and industrial means, but also by habitat sufficiency as well as by what we would today call natural capital and human capital, the modern age offers to realize a utopia of human fulfillment. Yet with our desires oblivious to all but the 'sumptuous garnitures of Life,' we have 'forgotten to *live* in the middle of them.' This paradox, in which existential life may be at once real or unreal, metaphorical or literal, points to the question of what constitutes the human itself. In the Romantic view of modern economic ideology, the satisfactions and fulfillments of human existence have been so severely occluded that the species survives only anaesthetically, only liminally human, numb to satisfaction and dead to life. The desire to 'really live,' as if this could not be taken for granted, is as much a commonplace of modern life as it is a bizarre symptom. When the category of human existential life becomes articulated as a metaphor and a project or plot, the doors fall open to the post-human imagination. The Romantic radicals prepare the way for modernists who will similarly refuse the modern narrative of economic progress (growth in property production yields flowering of welfare production), and will similarly try to disrupt this historical narrative by attacking its structures of feeling and history with signs, icons, and images of alternative economic experiences. In the latter, however, the modernist revival of pre-modern pasts flows together with a new figuration of the post-human animal.

Style becomes the unexpected battleground for the modern economic imagination. On the one hand, modernists turn to the production of an individual – and emphatically independent, typically challenging if not difficult – style as the medium in which human common sense, and the common-sense human, will be 'made new.' On the other hand, style already belongs to the world of fashion in which, Xenos argues, modern scarcity is defined: what is scarce is not only what is rare, but also what a consumer elite wants as a mark of distinction; and what the rest of us want is not, item by item, 'to possess what [these] others possess, but to imitate their style.' Style is the image of abundance. The commodity itself offers only a discrete, symbolic pleasure; the style it embodies, an imaginary, holistic satisfaction. Modern style appears self-sufficient, unruffled, unlaboured, cool. Were it to appear contingent or incomplete, to be worked or to require work, or to hold anything in reserve or require reserves from the consumer, its enchantment would be destroyed. Moreover, from the late nineteenth century forward, the rise of commodity and advertising display behind shop-front glass, beneath department store domes, radiant with electric lighting, and later, itself composed of electric, electronic, and digital imagery, created for the commodity an 'integrated world of illumination and animation' seamlessly woven into modern daily life.[4] These commodity worlds are unified by competing or interlocking styles, whose corporate icon will, as the twentieth century progresses, become the 'brand identity' (e.g., that of Nike, Coca-Cola, Disney, Microsoft, or DuMaurier) which imaginatively synthesizes, as belonging to kindred values and tastes, a diverse range of produced events, goods, and services. Style is a fantasy habitat, a mirage clinging to consumer abundance that renders the conditions of actual habitat and natural production invisible. In the hands of modernists, style must be rescued from this cursed enchantment: if style must be a fantasy habitat, mediated at some point by the commodity, let it be one that defies easy inhabitation. Let it be disorienting, difficult, or disturbing. Let it divert identification from the serene reification of unlaboured style as the image of welfare, and divert emulation from anthropocentric fetish. Let it demand, in its very consumption, the production of a post-human circuitry of desire, a desire routed through metaphors and icons of habitat, consumer, welfare, and natural production. In so doing, let it require work. Let it reveal its own contingency in time, place, and body, its own insufficiency of meaning, value, or closure, its own act of production as writing and reading.

Modernist writing that challenged conventional thought and feeling by rerouting desire through diverse economic modes and feelings generally followed one of two paths, either representing a threatening, unresolved problem in modern life, or venturing towards a utopian alternative. On both paths walks what I will call, for simplicity's sake, the stylized *creature*: a deconstructive synthesis of the human and the animal in an icon of alternative humanity living its heterodox relationship to nature, commodity, welfare, and habitat. The *problem creature*, grasped immediately as a problem of style, and gendered feminine, has an archetype in the watershed fin-de-siècle novel by H.G. Wells, *The Island of Dr. Moreau* (1896). Wells imagines a medical researcher who inhabits an obscure, deserted Pacific island in order to create, using radical vivisection techniques, new creatures neither animal nor human. A practical Nietzschean, this Dr Moreau has no moral purpose but a creative will to power – to push the limits of what he can do, what he can sculpt, in the medium of the living, thinking organism. His aesthetic drive is registered allegorically in his name, which echoes that of the painter Gustave Moreau, whose *Oedipus and the Sphinx* (1864), featuring a cat woman locked to Oedipus's breast, mirroring his cool gaze, tacitly posing the famous riddle of man. The vanguard creature in Moreau's laboratory is also a cat woman, but unlike to the myth, Moreau, bent on creative power alone, has no answer to the riddle of man beyond the self-sufficient mirage of his own productive power, and is destroyed by her.

Referring to this creature fashioned from a puma, Moreau says: 'The thing before you is no longer an animal, a fellow-creature, but a problem. Sympathetic pain – all I know of it I remember as a thing I used to suffer from years ago. I wanted – it was the only thing I wanted – to find out the extreme limit of plasticity in a living shape.'5 The revelation of biophysical plasticity, according to which any creature may be physically and psychologically transformed into another, is the heart of the modern problem posed here by Wells. This problem horrified many of his first readers, who found its deconstruction of a divinely sanctioned chain of being perverse and indecent.6 But for Wells biopolitics, not theology, is the problem. And the novel's biopolitics are not merely negative, as Moreau's tyranny may otherwise suggest. A utopian dimension glimmers ambivalently from Moreau's indifference to conventional pleasures and comforts. He is not only the would-be master of human plasticity, the liberator of human and animal life into an indistinct, creaturely future. He is not only, in his purely aesthetic will to power, a bizarre yet ominously prescient master of style. In channelling his own desires and those of his creatures away from the consumer production of the world from which he has all but severed himself (significantly, the major plot turn occurs with the breaking of a dietary restriction), he is a curious, new icon of primitive asceticism in his own right – one that unexpectedly allies him with the austere life of his island creatures. The power of this animalized icon ran deep with Wells: he took the name Jaguar, and Rebecca West, Panther, in their love affair from 1913 to 1924 – names their biographer Gordon Ray says 'stood for the whole attitude towards life evolved' by them. Panther and Jaguar 'emphasized the ruthless withdrawal from society that the relationship entailed, the fact that Rebecca and Wells were not part of the pack and did not acknowledge its law. Instead [as Wells put it], they were "carnivores" living apart in their hidden "lair," going forth to "catch food," and meeting "at the trodden place in the jungle."'[7] Thus Wells liked to play his own Moreau, remaking his identity on the model of Moreau's ultimate feline creation.

Moreau, adapted to this primitive lifestyle, lives supremely indifferent to the modern scarcity that is still felt by his disciple, Montgomery, and the shipwrecked narrator. Montgomery, like Moreau a figure of transgressive desire, but of conventional degeneracy rather than eccentric productivity, is compensated for his exile from modern abundance by the comforts of his homosexual bond with M'ling, a creature who performs all the domestic services of a wife for him, whom he affectionately recognizes as the only being to have 'ever really cared for him.' This gendering of the human-animal breakdown as a breakdown of sexual difference is intensified, interestingly, in the only modern-period film adaptation of the novel, *Island of Lost Souls* (1933; see fig. 2.1). This film has the same troubled reception as its parent novel: it was banned in England for being 'against nature.' ('Of course it's against nature,' parried actress Elsa Lanchester: 'So's Mickey Mouse.') The resonance

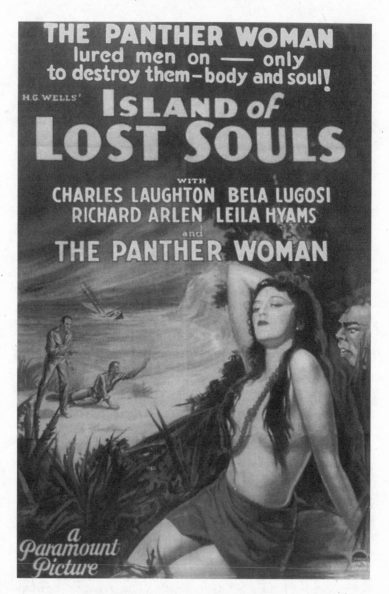

2.1 Poster for *Island of Lost Souls*, Paramount, 1933.

of Moreau's ambiguous artistry with that of modern comics is developed in British comics writer Alan Moore's adaptation of Wells's stories, in which Moreau appears as the renegade creator of Mother Goose, Puss 'n Boots, Rupert Bear, Babar, the river animals from *The Wind in the Willows*, Jimmy Swinnerton's cartoon tiger, and other iconic inhabitants, old and new, of the early twentieth century.[8] But the Paramount film adaptation may have disturbed audiences for its erotic as well as theological implications. Charles Laughton's Moreau combines the effeminate homosexuality of Wells's Montgomery and the cool superiority of Wells's Moreau. But in combining both to create a sensational villain, the film loses the moral ambiguity that is at the heart of the novel's apocalyptic anxieties about the contingency of human life as such upon the juggernaut of modern biophysical productive power. Wells presents Montgomery's transgressive feelings in a sympathetic if abject light, and views Moreau's work as amorally dedicated to science, as if to suggest that the plasticity of human life justifies no essential morality as to human-animal distinctions, gender identities, or sexual preferences. Only pain, viewed as the by-product of mere style, is intolerable – for whatever creature – and for this Moreau must pay. The Paramount film simplifies the matter by rendering the unified Montgomery-Moreau evil, though perhaps rather fascinatingly so, and by resolving Wells's biopolitical anxiety in the wish-fulfillment of a heterosexual romance (hence the cat woman – ironically, for Wells, renamed the Panther woman – serves in the film as a love interest for the shipwrecked hero). For Wells the deconstruction of gender and animal differences is simply the result of a creature that is a 'problem' rather than a definite thing. To see the creature in this light requires removal, in *The Island of Dr. Moreau*, to a different sort of scarcity – a scarcity of consumer production *tout court*. But to this 'problem' creature, Wells's story offers no solution.

Moreau's island may perhaps be seen as a fable that illustrates the contention of philosopher Giorgio Agamben, developed in *Homo Sacer*, that power over 'bare life' is a singularly modern compulsion, with a uniquely oppressive and violent, modern history. Via the laboratory crucible in which mere life, animal life, and human identity are dissolved into each other and remade, in what the creatures call his House of Pain, Wells's sovereign Moreau produces his island creature habitat the same way that, for Agamben, modern biopolitics produces its state citizenship, in a type of concentration camp with shifting, permeable borders, in which the production and recognition of a normative humanity might at any moment become exceptional, or the exceptional normative. Wells's message, in anticipation of Agamben, is to direct attention towards the political force and nature of the modern production of the human-animal borderline (what Agamben calls bare life), an activity that can only be glimpsed if we widen our view of political economy beyond consumer and welfare production to include habitat and natural production. This message is more starkly delivered in Wells's *The War of the Worlds* (1898), in which Martians take over the Earth, easily vanquishing human military opposition, until they are unexpectedly destroyed by putrefactive and viral bacteria, acting on their own, to which humans have acquired resistance. The plot twist of *War of the Worlds*, then, simply exploits the modern reader's habitual forgetfulness or repression of their own habitat production, of which bacteria are a parasitical member, and mocks the desperate feeling that, with humanity under threat, only the production of some ultimate weapon, the right industrial good, could save them. (Wells is no doubt recalling the great influenza pandemic of 1889–90, which would return in 1918.)

As a satirist, Wells goes further. The theme of *War of the Worlds* is the subjection of modern humanity to a global biopolitical power that reduces it to bare life, eerily both recalling the House of Pain and foreseeing the Nazi camps. After a period of hiding, the narrator emerges upon a landscape that is now a Martian habitat and feels what it may be like to be a nonhuman animal in a human habitat: 'For that moment I touched an emotion beyond the common range of men, yet one that the poor brutes we dominate know only too well. I felt as a rabbit might feel returning to his burrow and suddenly confronted by the work of a dozen busy navies digging the foundations of a house. I felt the first inkling of a thing that presently grew quite clear in my mind, that oppressed me for many days, a sense of dethronement, a persuasion that I was no longer a master, but an animal among animals, under the Martian heel. With us it would be as with them, to lurk and watch, to run and hide; the fear and empire of man had passed away.'⁹ Indeed, the possibilities are worse, for a fellow survivor speculates that humans will be raised in captivity as a food source. And here, a satiric twist sweeps the Martian romance aside as a mere allegory for the human production of bare life:

> All these – the sort of people that lived in these houses, and all those damn little clerks that used to live down that way – they'd be no good [to live in the wild, free of the Martians]. They have no proud dreams and no proud lusts; and a man who hasn't one or the other – Lord! What is he but funk and precautions? They just used to skedaddle off to work – I've seen hundreds of 'em, but of breakfast in hand, running wild and shining to catch their little season-ticket train, for fear they'd get dismissed if they didn't; working at businesses they were afraid to take the trouble to understand; skedaddling back for fear they wouldn't be in time for dinner; keeping indoors after dinner for fear of the back-streets, and sleeping with the wives they married, not because they wanted them, but because they had a bit of money that would make for safety in their one little miserable skedaddle through the world. Lives insured and a bit invested for fear of accidents. And on Sundays – fear of the hereafter. As if hell was built for rabbits! Well, the Martians will just be a godsend to these. Nice roomy cages, fattening food, careful breeding, no worry. After a week or so chasing about the fields and lands on empty stomachs, they'll come and be caught cheerful.

No need to wait for Martians to make humans into rabbits, when humans have already made rabbits of each other, and of rabbits. The choice of a rabbit figure to emblemize modern bare life is ironic, transforming a conventional symbol of fertility or natural production into that of consumer production – a creature of submission to the commodity world and to the generalized fear sustained by generalized scarcity, a creature that has forgotten or repressed other desires that speak in dreams and lusts. As for Carlyle, the question of what constitutes human life brutally invades everyday modernity. In confused answer to the riddle of itself, the new problem creature drifts in a sea of post-human wonder, freedom, horror, and pity.

This problem, considered as general to modernity, has a rich tradition in science fiction after Wells, whose milestones include the genetic dystopia of Aldous Huxley's *Brave New World* (1932), and, more recently, the pandemic apocalypse engineered by a self-styled Moreau in Margaret Atwood's *Oryx and Crake* (2003). But the problem is not only general, which is to say, restricted to the expression of a universalized, disaffected patriarchal experience of the consumer economy – the feeling registered in Wells's allegory of male rabbits, in the crowd of male living dead that are the rabbits' kin in Eliot's *The Waste Land*, or in the creatures' abject catechism on Moreau's island, 'Are we not Men?'[10] For some sectors of society, as suggested earlier, modern abundance never became fully realizable and hence credible, and the violence of biopolitical power could be directly felt. Such conditions reveal themselves, for example, in the stories of Jean Rhys, along axes of racial oppression, class poverty, and sexism and the social inequality of women. In 'The Mannequin' (1927), a young expatriate woman in Paris is driven by poverty to seek work as a fashion model, despite the low pay and ill repute of the profession. In the front rooms of the business, she sits or walks before the 'raking eyes' of buyers, surrounded by opulent décor, learning 'to wear the innocent and springlike air and garb of the jeune fille.' Her person dissolves into her clothes, and her clothes into her person, as a fashion category (the jeune fille), an icon in the lexicon of style to be emulated by consumers. Yet behind the scenes, the mannequin – her dehumanization into a problem creature crafted by her employer's Moreau-like domination, frankly marked in the story's title – enters a world of 'unexpected somberness,' a 'rabbit warren' connected by 'dark passages,' and with a 'dingy and melancholy' aspect. 'Dressed in the black cotton, chemise-like garment of the mannequin off-duty,' she finds her way to the 'underground' lunch room:

> She was in a big, very low-ceilinged room, all the floor space occupied by long wooden tables with no cloths ... She was sitting at the mannequins' table, gazing at a thick and hideous white china plate, a twisted tin fork, a wooden-handled stained knife, a tumbler so thick it seemed unbreakable.
>
> There were twelve mannequins at Jeanne Veron's: six of them were lunching, the others still paraded, goddess-like, till their turn came for rest and refreshment. Each of the twelve was a distinct and separate type: each of the twelve knew her type and kept to it, practicing rigidly in clothing, manner, voice and conversation.

The oppressive production of these women as creatures of style, their reduction like dolls or animals to the margins of bare life in order to do so, and their subservience to a master designer, together offer a striking realist counterpart to Wells's fantasy of Moreau. Their stark, prison-like habitat and drab uniform clothing echo Agamben's claim that the camp is the paradigm of modern biopolitical power. Throughout her stories, Rhys presents women in similarly oppressed circumstances, but offers no alternative life for them. In 'Hunger,' the impoverished speaker tells us that whenever she goes five days without food, she loses her usual needs and desires and takes pleasure in intangibles of the moment: 'Anything: lovely words, or the sound of a concertina from the street: even a badly played piano can make one cry. Not with hunger or sadness. No! But with the extraordinary beauty of life.'[11] But this pleasure is ephemeral, lived on the very edge, near the negation of life, and the problem of the modern creature in its unequal gradient across the classes and sexes remains painfully inescapable.

Yet another tendency among modernist writers is to bring forth utopian experiences of needs and desires, scarcity and abundance, alternative to the hollow reign of consumer abundance and the frightening revelation of our habitat production that it conceals. Its icon will similarly be the ambiguous, posthuman creature of style, in which human, animal, and even technological traces are unified. But this utopian creature has solved its problem, and bears no riddle – unless it is the generic utopian dilemma of its realization in history.

Such utopian creatures may be found, in rare isolated portraiture, amid the poetic bestiary of Marianne Moore. In 'The Jerboa,' Moore contrasts the material opulence of human civilizations with the spare habitat of a desert rat, finding a truly satisfying 'abundance,' as opposed to consumer 'plenty,' in the ascetic life and sensual style of the latter. The little jerboa 'has happiness' in its 'shining silver house // of sand. O rest and / joy, the boundless sand, / the stupendous sand-spout, / no water, no palm-trees, no ivory bed, / tiny cactus; but one would not be he / who has nothing but plenty.' Yet the poem does not celebrate a wealth that is, in the tradition of the desert anchorite, transcendental, and even contrasts the jerboa to Jacob, who dreamed of a ladder reaching out of the desert. The animal's abundance is in a body and habitat that allow it to live in sensuality and grace, and nearly all the verses devoted to it are descriptive, in such a way that the formally unique and graceful style of the poem is experienced as the style of the animal: 'By fifths and sevenths, / in leaps of two lengths, / like the uneven notes / of the Bedouin flute, it stops its gleaning / on little wheel castors, and makes fern-seed / foot-prints with kangaroo speed.'[12] In Moore's poems, content and form, animal and *techne*, merge in the perfect cyborgian unity that is only purely seen in modern comics and animation figures like Krazy Kat or Donald Duck. For this writer, in a peculiar sense, animals *are* style, but style as habitat production, rather than a species of goods. Hence the animal Moore chooses as an exemplum of style itself, in 'To a Snail,' is another ascetic icon (here of 'compression'), but one that produces and carries its home, rather than a mere adornment, attached to its body. It should come as no surprise that she referred to her poems themselves as animals. Insofar as poems are human, or animated by human apprehension, by organs of hand, eyes, ears, breath, Moore's theriomorphic image for the poem is more than a cute metaphor, the emblem for a diminutive, devalued, pet form of modern literature; rather, it is literal, denoting an animal writing produced against anthropocentric economies of meaning. Here, style is not the language of a fantasy or deferred habitat to be sought through consumer production, but an alternative language of abundance which asks us to identify with the animal and its ascetic activity, while enjoying its mere and explicit act of living in a unique body and place, just as we simultaneously enjoy, in the verses quoted above, a mere and explicit act of reading. Conversely, bad style is evident in art apprehended fantastically as having its own, reified life, both plunged in mysterious depths apart from economies of human production and exchange, and readily appropriated to human vanity: 'They have imposed on us ...,' complains the eloquent cat regarding its human keepers in 'The Monkeys,' '... saying / it is not for us to understand art; finding it / all so difficult, examining the thing // as if it were inconceivably arcanic ... / ... malignant / in its power over us and deeper / than the sea when it proffers flattery in exchange for hemp, / rye, flax, horses, platinum, timber, and fur.'[13] Moore's animal writing offers a utopian indifference to such anthropocentric flattery and the biophysical violence – a cargo of resources, animal, plant, and mineral, united only by commodification (in exchange) and modern consumption (in the depthless maw of the sea) – that it conceals.

Such utopian icons run also through modernist fiction. One in particular has drawn much recent comment by critics interested in animal representation: the aloof, powerful horse in D.H. Lawrence's eponymous novella, *St. Mawr* (1925). Phonetically synonymous with the martyred author of *Utopia* (canonized a decade later), St Mawr also represents an outcaste life, an ascetic ideal, and one that is post-humanist in being simply and mysteriously *more* than human: an animal otherness whose vitality is somehow 'more real' than human society to the novel's heroine, yet paradoxically, also more valuable to her humanity.[14] In this story, a young American woman in England falls in love with a horse who represents physical and spiritual satisfaction missing from her bourgeois social milieu. Lou's relationship to the horse, whom she rescues from a plot to geld, occasions what is effectively a separation from her husband, and a return to the American Southwest of her family heritage. There, she and St Mawr part company, each liberated by the other, and by a wilderness margin in America, to live as they wish. For St Mawr, this life is the expanse and sensual activity of the working ranch, as opposed to the English breeding business and its product of social riding. When she is still immersed in the latter milieu, the heroine needs St Mawr as a symbol and possession, a commodity with the aura of an alternative kind of desire and satisfaction. By the end of the story, she no longer needs either the property or the symbol, and can let him go. And St Mawr no longer needs her.

Yet the horse has taught her a lesson about her own animal and human – or rather post-human – nature, which she will ultimately live via an ascetic withdrawal from commodity satisfactions. After complaining to her mother that the 'animal' in men has either been tamed or 'gone queer and wrong,' and her mother mocks her for idealizing the primitive animal man, Lou rejects this primitivism: 'I don't consider the cave man is a real human animal at all. A pure animal man would be as lovely as a deer or a leopard, burning like a flame fed straight from underneath. And he'd be part of the unseen, like a mouse is, even. And he'd never cease to wonder, he'd breathe silence and unseen wonder, as the partridges do, running in the stubble. He'd be all the animals in turn, instead of one, fixed, automatic thing, which he is now, grinding on the nerves.'[15] Lawrence does not advocate mimicry of an idealized animal otherness; we are not supposed, as Lou is not supposed, to wish to be a horse like St Mawr, or to discover some essential horse within. Nor to be some essential animal man, the fantasy of an historical or habitat regression. Lawrence is equally acerbic regarding the social life of frontier Americans as of urban Europeans.

Rather, the human animal realizes itself, and enjoys wonder, in its very plasticity, the creative subjection of its nature to history. This plasticity is figured in the modernist re-appropriation of style as the mirror of habitat production as opposed to habitat consumption. Hence the truth hidden in the cliché of the modernist as individual genius: marking in style an individual responsibility for habitat production, a *genius locus*.

The narrative lesson of St Mawr circles back to the self-reflexive linguistic technology of Moore's animals in a later novella by Kay Boyle, *The Crazy Hunter* (1940), which is also about an independently spirited horse rescued from violence by an independently spirited young woman. In this story, the horse, Brigand, is struck with blindness and, being similarly unsuited for the breeding business, is condemned to death. The young woman appeals to her father, Candy, an alcoholic who has left the running of the farm to her mother, when she brings him a letter from an Irish friend who suggests that Brigand be employed in farm work rather than destroyed. She finds him reading:

> Candy had been by the morning bus to Pellton and bought two detective stories in paper covers at Woolworth's shop in Fore Street, and he sat on the veranda in the fan-backed Indian arm-chair reading *Wanton Killing* in mild, soft-shaven, immaculately accoutred peace (because this would kill the hours of the afternoon and a portion of the evening, this story that did not for an instant deal with people but with the familiarly stamped counterfeits of detective, family, doctor, corpse). On the corner of the ping-pong table lay the other, *Murder in Hand*, still clean and marvelously unread (instrument lying in readiness to slug tomorrow afternoon and evening in their turn into timeless insensibility).[16]

In the foreground of this passage is the layered irony of Candy's consumption of pulp fiction to murder time, which will obscure and allow him to forget his passive complicity in the murder of the horse. The consumption of violence veils the violence of habitat. On another level is the connection between this form of literary consumption and Candy's alcoholism: both are symptoms of the failure of modern abundance to satisfy, and both represent a commodity that escapes the scarcity-abundance spiral of desires and needs, trading welfare for abject oblivion (or counting abject oblivion as the only real welfare). This pulp fiction is 'counterfeit' because it has no currency, no value in the economy of production exposed by the novella. On a further level is the biopolitical paradigm that identifies the violence against the animal with colonialism (the manufactured 'peace' of the Indian veranda, in contrast to the authentically anti-violent stance of the Irish friend). The self-reflexivity of the passage demands that *The Crazy Hunter* be judged against a 'counterfeit' style, demands that we recognize that unlike *Wanton Killing*, it does 'deal with people,' here including Brigand, and that time spent consuming the novella may be apprehended as a type of production to be measured against Candy's pure consumerism, and may be situated, like his, in the suppressed habitat in which each reader is embedded and at work.

Unlike in Moore's poems, the personified animals of Lawrence's and Boyle's fictions are not protagonists. However potent they are as icons of the authors' radical visions and as agents of change in their protagonists, we do not enter into their lives and habitat except in flashes that illuminate their suppressed consubstantiality with our own. It is rare in modern fiction for an animal figure to be the protagonist of a narrative in this sense – or rather, in verbal fiction. In the graphic narrative tradition whose birth and development, from the turn of the nineteenth century on, coincide with modernism and its aftermaths, the personified animal is a common type. Typical, too, is its utopian expression of a different economic reality – one of apparent scarcity, which is of modern consumer production, and one of alternative welfare, of an often magical or wondrous pleasure in habitat production: the plastic selves and mutable worlds of Disney and countless other comics and film animation creatures. Typical again, is their posthuman creatureliness. We find such a creature the protagonist of the most celebrated comic strip of the modern age, George Herriman's *Krazy Kat* (1913–44), reputed to have been read by Gertrude Stein, Ernest Hemingway, Pablo Picasso, Edmund Wilson, e e cummings, Louis Zukofsky, and T.S. Eliot.[17] In this anthropomorphic animal strip widely syndicated by Hearst, a carefree cat, Krazy, is in love with a scornful mouse, Ignatz, whose compulsive pleasure is to throw bricks at the cat's head. The missiles are interpreted by the cat as love messages, while the mouse is soberly punished by a watchful dog, Offissa Pupp. This narrative cycle is the basis upon which Herriman played thousands of variations, daily and weekly, over thirty years of the strip's run. The racial and sexual ambiguity of the Kat, and the modernist aesthetics of language, narrative, and image in the strip, were evident to contemporary fans (indeed, the strip was adapted to jazz ballet, with a comics libretto by Herriman, in 1922) and have drawn renewed attention from cultural historians and literary scholars today.[18] The Kat, like other funny animal figures in popular comics and animated cartoons, is a stylistically unified synthesis of the human and the animal in a creature that is both and neither. Herriman's graphic style stands out among Golden Age cartoonists for an erratic, scratchy, sketchy line always on the verge of falling apart into a stumble of cross-hatches or tangle of jarring squiggles. The absorption of the figure into style is a familiar modernist project, and its effects here are particularly striking, where it asserts the fragile material identity of its beings from panel to panel. The very identifiability of creatures and of actions follows a razor's edge along Herriman's ecstatically hasty, insistently unmasterful line. The same applies to settings, panels, and layout, which morph surrealistically across the narratives held together by his creatures. The setting is an imaginary desert in Kokonino Kounty, a stark world based on the American Southwest much loved by Herriman, where native icons like cactuses, buttes, Joshua trees, pueblo houses, and kivas emerge from and vanish into the blank, fertile surface of the page along with palm trees, giraffes, clock towers, and Chinese laundries. As with images, so with words.

The Kat's dialect is synthetic, a seamless, be-bop blend of part-languages that evoke an array of Englishes, and becomes its own. 'OY, "IGNATZ." !!! WHERE FOUR IS THOU, IGNATZ ? [...] OI, WOI IS ME WOI IS ME,' complains Krazy in a 1925 episode, when a seal unexpectedly flops by. 'MY GOO-NISS SAKES, L'IL SILL – WIDOW GOEST THOU AT?'[19]

But this paper-and-ink desert with its strangely juxtaposed fragments of language, culture, and creature does not pose the nihilist problems of Eliot's own waste land; rather, it answers them. The Kat is a creature of ineradicable sympathy, goodwill, and fun. And of abundance – without reference to consumer production. The latter is present both negatively, in a fantasy desert habitat traversed by creature flaneurs and subject only to erratic and singular manufacture of goods; and positively, in the one icon of consumer production, the rigid, uniform bricks produced for Ignatz to fire at Krazy's head, to obtain an ever-elusive satisfaction. The abundance to which Ignatz is blind, but in which Krazy revels, is found in the creative plasticity of the Kokonino world. In one episode, when Krazy finds a solitary coconut palm, she/he obtains balloons from a wandering salesman and uses glue, oakum, and paint to counterfeit 'a child coconut or two' so the tree will be 'heppier with his lonesim sitiwation' (see colour plate 6).[20] Here Herriman's playful subversions of what Giorgio Agamben calls the anthropological machine run rampant.[21] The tree itself is paradoxically and at once both suggestively anthropomorphized and insistently inhuman, which perhaps accounts for its uncanny appeal. Graphically, it has no animal or human features, and so lacks the essential convention of living being in comics, according to Scott McCloud the basis of human identification, a face.[22] Yet when first introduced, its fronds are shedding iconic tears. The caption reads: 'with only the shifting sands, the dancing dunes, and the echoing cliffs of kaibito to keep him company a coconut tree grown to pulsating palmhood grieves for the parent grove in coconino – and silently sheds a modest nostalgian tear –.' The final fusion of modesty and nostalgia nudges us beyond the tree's animalization to a human personification, but only precariously. In most of the following panels, we only see its inexpressive lower trunk (which perspective is identified with Krazy in panel 7), while what we have been taught to recognize as its 'head' is out of sight. There are two exceptions: in the first, a central panel shows the balloon-coconuts just attached by Krazy, and the lack of teardrop icons seems to imply that the tree is 'heppier,' as four 'coconut' faces now stare out from it; in the second, Ignatz has chopped through the trunk in order to steal the coconuts while Krazy is asleep beneath, and the iconic tears reappear – but these could be either renewed tears of sorrow or the more ambiguous 'anxiety' sweat icons also conventional to comics (without a face, impossible to tell).[23] The contrast between Ignatz's selfish and objectifying view of the coconuts and Krazy's own sentiment frames the delightful implication at the heart of the story: the tree need not be fooled by the fake coconuts for these surrogate children to have the value Krazy intends. For the Kat has laboriously made them, produced them as 'children' of his/her idiosyncratic activity and imagination, and given them to the tree as a gift; they embody Krazy's relation to the tree, his/her sympathy for another, however inscrutable and ambiguous, Kokonino being. This bond is emphasized by seven panels showing the Kat's head affectionately resting against the trunk. As the strip progresses, therefore, we are drawn away from the narrative problems to enjoy the birth in recognition of an abundance of unexpected lives, and the satisfaction of bonds of kinship and shared habitat production involving them. Whereas in classical economics, work is mere biophysical machinery required to produce the value of the commodity, here the situation undergoes a utopian reversal: the commodity, whether the balloon or Krazy's production of it as a coconut child, has no value except as the requisite vehicle of satisfying work.

Herriman's Kokonino, like the animal worlds of Moore, Lawrence, and Boyle, rejects modern consumer abundance and seeks pleasure in the imagination of a scarcity of commodities themselves. Cartoon figures, like these other poetic creatures, are identified by their activity rather than their property, and their desires and needs are always aligned ultimately and strictly with activity rather than consumption, so that even icons of consumption – like the hamburger-obsessed Wimpey in E.C. Segar's *Thimble Theatre* (1919–38) – are likely to be, like Ignatz, satirical figures of dead-ended desire and irresponsible agency. Like ascetic exercises, these figures offer a fantasy – or a lesson – of how to be satisfied with doing rather than having.[24] Indeed, the imaginative exercise of doing abundantly, in the economic light of satisfying needs and desires, while having little or less, is shared by such diverse modernist deserts as we find in *The Waste Land*, *Four Saints in Three Acts*, *St. Mawr*, and *Krazy Kat*, and is emblemized in the counter-culture tradition of bohemia which persists into the present day. Today, where such utopian worlds and creatures still gleam with a strange economic light is where they have rejected a too-easy primitivism – the fantasy of a world without commodities, without property, without technological manufacture, or without communal diversity and conflict – and where the otherness of the human as an animal bound to its habitat, not only for survival but for welfare, is insistently recognized. These texts, now marooned on the shores of a modern commodity scarcity their creators had never imagined, bear the same lessons with a new urgency. Perhaps by thinking what it means to identify with – and enjoy identifying with – a Krazy Kat or a stylish snail or a Saint Ten, we will unlock the structures of feeling we may need if we are to survive the future of our increasingly small planet.

Chapter Three

Surviving History

Against the bitter harvest of modern economic life, out of which it is born, the creative desert of *Krazy Kat* evokes desires to live otherwise, and in a dream of renunciation and asceticism that imagines new industries of warmth and delight, to be modern otherwise. But we humans are not cartoon kats, it must hardly be said, and cannot change ourselves and history with a cartoonist's tabula rasa and graphic genius. This dream lives on into many forms of contemporary art and literature, but so does the problem of making it real, of telling a story that gets us from where we are to the Kokonino County of our dreams. This is the stuff of romance, whether realist or otherwise, the quest for a new order of things.

Contemporary narrative that takes up this problem may stray very little from its modernist archetype: the quest may simply negate the conventional modern economy and assert the power of an individual or collective withdrawal and re-creation. All animalized superheroes fall into this category – Batman, Spiderman, Wolverine, and others who, like Stein's saints, thrive in a niche habitat, always somehow monastic, apart from, yet in, the interstices of the worlds they must renounce in order to be who they become. In these more sensational niche habitats, the fantasy centres on work – how to live a satisfying life that not only refuses the mediocre satisfactions of modern consumption but of modern labour (work as commodity) – and the utopian work of justice, in sovereign violence, that alone offers these post-human creatures a sense of abundance. The quest narrative for such figures is the 'origin story,' the story of transformation from normal to new life that has always held a special fascination and value among comics readers. Such ascetic quests are generic fantasy and, in subordinating realist possibility to wish fulfillment, cannot tell us much about the problem of historical realization. Closer in spirit to *Krazy Kat*, with the same narrative of direct, fantasy negation, is Jim Davis's *Garfield* (from 1978). Garfield embodies a kind of pleasure principle and ascetic satisfaction akin to Krazy's, and has inherited a modernist ironic genius, but he inhabits a realist domestic space that dangles before us the tempting vision that such economic reincarnation is humanly possible. Garfield is like us a consumer, but only of an impossibly narrow range of goods – principally lasagna and television programming – that is uncannily commensurate with the limited consumer lives, if not tastes, of actual cats. He is happy with very little, without being in any way feline primitivist. Yet behind his other pleasure – laziness – lurks the same anxiety that permeates superhero fantasy. Garfield is an animal who does not labour, and indeed rejects work altogether. The realism of Davis's economic imagination evaporates in this impossibility of negating both modern labour and work more generally (unless the idiosyncratic Garfield masks a rather mundane modern desire, a sentimental image of retirement). One of the more elaborate narratives of modernist renunciation is Jeff Smith's graphic narrative, *Bone* (1992–3), in which the hero is an icon of the starkest reduction of the creaturely to a metaphorical skeleton of plastic blankness, an animate bone, who travels into a land where money and labour are unknown, work belongs to systems of subsistence and barter, and the desire for consumer abundance has absurd and ruinous results. As will be seen, work turns out to be a central problem in all narratives that try to bridge the gap between historical and alternative modern economic lives.

While such modernist narratives of economic refusal may be subversive, the project to live otherwise, to create new structures of feeling for both scarcity and abundance, and thus to alter modern understandings of welfare, has since the 1960s taken another form: today modern scarcity may well be felt as less a matter for negation or refusal, than a condition for adaptation, a fate. No longer can we simply reject modern abundance in an act of culturalist enclosuring or renunciation: we are forced by the image of a small planet with finite resources to feel our economic life increasingly as a Faustian pact with natural history, rather than an anthropocentric conquering of it. The modernist heroics of choice give way to a postmodern awe before necessity.

A writer who moves back and forth seamlessly between these modernist and postmodern narrative registers – between quests of renunciation and adaptation, mediated by unexpected creatures, and with a fraught relationship to work – is Haruki Murakami. In *Kafka on the Shore* (2002), a teenage boy runs away from his wealthy home with a knapsack and a small sum of money, in part to escape his apparently loveless parent and empty school experience, and in part to escape the fate he believes, like Oedipus, has slated him to murder his father. A familiar modernist renunciation of modern wealth is played out as a destiny that entangles the histories of a number of people and animals initially unknown to each other. Work and consumption are central themes. The boy is able to find a job in an obscure private library, but this belongs more to barter and gift arrangements than to the marketplace: it is offered to him by a new friend as part of a growing relationship between them, and the work, which incidentally allows him to indulge his desire to read, is understood as an exchange for free accommodation in the library. The friend also invites him to stay in a wilderness cabin, where the boy lives in anchoritic retreat. While these characters live simply, their lives as consumers are represented in Murakami's attention to eating itself. The quotidian consumption of food is described in luxurious detail, and its methods of preparation reflected upon. If this were not embedded in a narrative of renunciation, it would seem hedonistic – but, as it is, it suggests an uncanny alternative to, rather than example of, conventional consumerist pleasure. Whereas D.H. Lawrence sought a sensualist asceticism in the example of aboriginal and animal lives he saw struggling to escape the net of modernity, Murakami seeks the same in modernity's own mundane modes of production and experience, in a sandwich as much as in a snake dance. This convergence is visible in the novel's parallel narrative of Nakata, a mentally injured, elderly man who is mysteriously able to speak with cats and is the actual murderer of the boy's father. The murder is enacted while the father appears to Nakata as a serial cat killer, and in the form of whisky icon Johnny Walker. This icon of an addictive substance as popular commodity, of chronically unsatisfied consumption as role model, is echoed in the figure of Colonel Sanders, chosen as a 'famous capitalist icon' to help Nakata elsewhere in the story.[1] Both commercial icons seem to come to life in order to enable human action between the world of the living and the world of the dead, and the Johnny Walker figure links modern consumption to a horrific genocide enacted upon animals. Equally important as mediators are cats themselves, and Nakata's ability as a kind of animalized human to speak with them, as their knowledge (and, in the murder, their suffering) plays a role in the conjunction of the characters' fates. In contrast to the dark or degraded symbolic burden of the commercial icons, then, the cats, the boy, and the elderly man all lead lives of reduced needs and enviable pleasures, indicating via a blurring of human-animal differences an alternative way of feeling about what one really needs to be happy. If it were not for the obsession with fate registered in the novel's self-reflexive mode of tragedy, a fate whose causes remain mysterious though intriguingly associated with capitalism, the novel would lean very much in the direction of individual renunciation and renewal, seducing its readers to a vision of lifestyle change based on dropping out of conventional society and its measure of needs and satisfactions. But it remains in suspense, bohemian without a bohemia, unsure of its meaning in relation to actual personal or historical change.[2]

In Murakami's less modernist novels, *A Wild Sheep Chase*

(1982) and *The Wind-Up Bird Chronicle* (1994–5), the narrative of individual renunciation and social withdrawal, together with an underworld journey plot, is more completely and challengingly reabsorbed into a narrative of adaptation to history and necessity. In both novels, the protagonist drops out of mainstream society and work in order to pursue a mysterious quest. In *Wild Sheep Chase*, as in *Kafka*, the climax of the quest occurs in a solitary rite of passage in a remote wilderness. What is so attractive about all these narratives is the idea of leaving conventional work behind, but still having work to do, work that is more satisfying; and the intensity of pleasure that only a very limited use of commodities, and property in particular, can bring. It is no surprise that creatures who bridge conventionally human and animal worlds are central to the mystery: the Sheep Man in *Wild Sheep Chase*, and the cats in *Kafka* and *Wind-Up Bird Chronicle*. But these are not romantic stories of revelation in nature. What each protagonist discovers in solitary withdrawal are invisible, often morbid webs of connection among others; what he uncovers in remote, inhuman nature is a buried history of human violence. Each narrative is about a fragile healing process that allegorizes the cure as a plunge at one and the same moment into the degraded animal and the concealed history of a modern habitat. In *Wind-Up Bird*, the search for a missing cat leads its owner to a deserted backyard with a deep well in it. The well, pitch dark at the bottom, becomes a strangely alluring if frightening retreat for the protagonist, doubling a well in the Manchurian desert fifty years earlier, which imprisons a soldier during the invasion of China. The isolation at the bottom of the wells – in both instances a product of traumatic modern history, a hidden destiny that reverberates morbidly, unacknowledged into the present – strips the human creature at its bottom of all but a threshold of needs and desires to live. Its darkness holds, in place of water, the terrifying fluidity or plasticity of the human animal, but in the same element, its difficult hope. Murakami deftly layers two narratives and two temporal periods that gradually converge – the first, in contemporary history, whose plot is centred in urban domestic life and involves a missing cat, a missing wife, various ghosts and strays, and the enigmatic history of a neighbouring residential property; the second, during the Second World War, involves an officer's traumatic experience of the imperialist military foray into China, a narrative whose unforgettable horror is the massacre by decree of animals in a Manchurian zoo, by reluctant soldiers who will themselves be abandoned to the bullets or concentration camps of the Soviet army. The resolution to this novel's healing narrative coincides with the return of the cat, 'a symbol of something good that grew up between' the protagonist and his wife, and, by extension, of fidelity to others with whom one · lives – whether human or non-human, stranger or kin, living or dead – who must be taken more care of.[3] Thus the vicissitudes of social directionlessness and alienation, felt in familiar domestic worlds of animals and kin, are moved from below by deeper currents of imperialist and military history. The former is the realm of modern economic culture and its modernist discontents; the latter is the realm of postmodern economic crisis – the conflict of an anthropocentric production of consumer abundance with a post-humanist experience of planetary scarcity – and its problem creatures. Between a cultivated taste for 'less' amid the richness of modern bourgeois life, and a fateful encounter with 'less' in the accumulating ruins and graves of that life's history, Murakami's narratives teeter precariously, uncertain of their lesson.

An illuminating contrast may be found in the more exemplary postmodern graphic narrative by Anders Nilsen, *Dogs and Water* (2007), in which the narrative of modernist renunciation is pared down to a minimum, and hard necessity and adaptation are in the foreground of a quest for an ineffable life goal or satisfaction. The story presents a solitary young man with knapsack and teddy bear journeying through a cold, desert waste – apparently rock or tundra – with virtually no vegetation, rare human encounters, and built structures few and far between and crumbled into ruins (see fig. 3.1). In this realm, consumer production has nearly vanished. The act of renunciation, of ascetic withdrawal or enclosure, is given in an opening

3.1 Anders Nilsen, *Dogs and Water* (Montreal: Drawn and Quarterly, 2007), p. 27. © 2007 Anders Nilsen.

reflection: 'Ever since we first started talking about doing this I've been open to it, even eager,' he tells his bear. 'Even when everyone said we'd starve, or freeze to death.'[4] But the journey is not evidently satisfying, and the landscape does not yield anything like the creative fertility of Kokonino.

As in McCay's and Herriman's work, things and creatures (if less frequently) suddenly appear out of the blankness of the panel/desert and vanish back into it, but seldom here without violence or alienation. For example, when the man meets a group of animals resembling caribou, he lets one of them sniff then lick him, opening himself to the creature's interest in him. When the animal suddenly butts him with its antlers, injuring his eye, while another bites into the teddy bear, the situation degenerates into an all-out fight that drives the animals away, remaining mysterious to him. His few encounters with humans, who are usually armed or victims of gunshots, and may speak languages unintelligible to each other, are similarly embedded in violence and alienation. Indeed, the decay of human society into fragments of suspicion or belligerence, the eerie desolation of the natural landscape, the scarcity of food, and ruined habitations, together appear more as conventional signs of a post-nuclear holocaust destiny than of some lightly populated hinterland in the present day. Hence the unsentimental desert in *Dogs and Water* is felt, despite an apparent act of choice by the man to inhabit it, to symbolize an inevitable condition of his historical world, the fateful scarcity of a small planet.

A crucial figure in the *Dogs and Water* habitat is the teddy bear, to whom the man's monologue throughout the story is addressed. Indeed, in listening in on the monologue, the reader is curiously aligned with the bear, surreptitiously taking its place. This is not hard to do in a comics world in which the cartoon icon of a teddy bear is virtually identical to that of many other personified bears with whom humans have had no trouble identifying, from the pioneering funny animals in Jimmy Swinnerton's *Little Bears and Tykes* (1895–7), to the immensely popular, still-produced comics icon of Rupert Bear created by Mary Tourtel (1920), to today's Winnie-the-Pooh, Care Bears, and innumerable manga pandas.[5] And, of course, outside the comics medium, the teddy bear has itself become the icon of a special kind of toy in North American life: the personified toy companion of small children. I will return to the matter of problem creatures and childhood identification in the last chapter of this book. At this point, what needs to be recognized is Nilsen's choice of a teddy bear as his protagonist's sole valued property, for it stands in sharp distinction to other kinds of valued possessions – those that would signify social status (the obsession of classical economic theorists from Adam Smith and David Hume forward), social power (as capital), individual satisfaction (as consumer power), or material sustenance and welfare – all of which are thin on the ground in Nilsen's imagined habitat. The teddy bear is detached here from any notion of a plaything, a toy (as is consistent with real life), and stands for an intensely personal relationship, somehow primary, more important to the man, and constitutive of him, than any other in the story. A Freudian reading would find in the teddy bear a transitional object, an object that exists on the frontier of distinctions between self and other. But that is not the signification here, where the adult man's bear is acknowledged simultaneously as another creature and as an inanimate thing, not as a narcissistic metaphor. How can this be possible? And how do we identify with that creature – that problem creature that is the unnamed bear – as readers bound to the man's voice and narrative as the bear is bound to the man's back?

The beginning of an answer may be found in Steve Baker's reading of the personified animal icon in comics, in which he observes that scholars of talking animal stories have typically denied the animal, treating its personified icon as a transparent sign for the purely human. On the contrary, he argues, the graphic icon of the animal form, even in the most anthropocentric of stories, carries its animal significations, working as a Derridean supplement against the grain of human exceptionalism: it is always also about the animal, and in an open, unresolved sense, about the human in uncertain relationship to the animal, as a problem creature that cannot be pinned down by taxonomies of human, racial, or gender hierarchy. This ambiguity of animal representation in comics is nowhere better expressed than in A.E. Bunser's graphic novella *Macintosh Booth* (2002), in which a personified larva is, like Babar the elephant, adopted as the protégé of an elderly woman, and similarly civilized. But the particularity of the larva is never quite lost, even when he sits at a desk in school or drinks tea. On the one hand, the larva figure is faceless. Our attention is directed by default to his body, a virtually legless, plump cylinder that defies anthropomorphic personification by the reader. On the other hand, in every panel featuring the larva, his figure appears in nearly the same aspect and posture, as if copied from one scene to the next, as if resisting an anthropomorphic expression of body movement and adaptation to environment. The effect is to set up between the verbal narrative, which insists on an anthropomorphic Bildungsroman for the larva, and the graphic image, which insists on the non-human temporality, body, and even interior mystery of the larva as larva, a productive dilemma: we can neither simply personify the animal as *one of us*, nor simply animalize it as an insignificant being, but are left opening out into some other life world that is in-between. The ending, which I will not disclose, foregrounds this mystery in a contemplation of the creature's agency.

In order to move a step closer to an understanding of the peculiarity of identification with such problem creatures, I read Baker's work through the lens of Donna Haraway's work on companion species, in which she argues that all creatures, even those that are sculpted in stone or digitized on screen, are figures of technological and biological encounters, the living traces of real inter- or intra-species genealogies.[6] Such naturalcultural complexity flows in the lines of Nilsen's teddy bear. In the stark landscape of this story, it has obviously been a commodity, something once produced for the market, now but one among a man's few similarly manufactured possessions (clothes, survival gear). Like these it is no longer a commodity, but has its value in uses detached from its market history. Its use value, however, is a curious one unfamiliar to economic

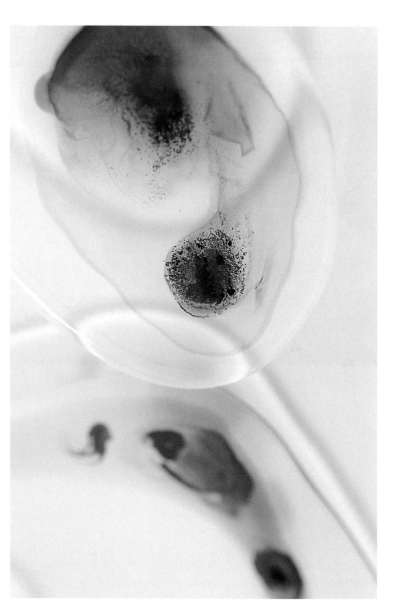

Plate 1 Rui Pimenta, *that subtle knot which makes us human*, 2009. Resin, latex, and ink on Plexiglas. Collection of the artist.

Plate 2 Paul Gauguin, *Te Rerioa* (The Dream), 1897. Oil on canvas.
Courtauld Institute Galleries, London. © The Samuel Courtauld
Trust, The Courtauld Gallery, London.

Plate 3 Winsor McCay, detail from *Little Nemo in Slumberland*,
New York Herald, 15 October 1905.

Plate 4 Takashi Murakami (Japanese, 1962–), *The World of Sphere*, 2003.
Acrylic on canvas mounted on board, 3500 × 3500 mm (2 panels).
© 2003 Takashi Murakami/Kaikai Kiki Co., Ltd. All Rights Reserved.

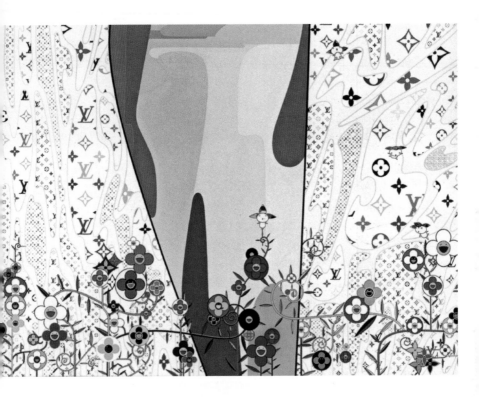

Plate 5 Takashi Murakami (Japanese, 1962–), *The World of Sphere*, 2003 (detail).
Acrylic on canvas mounted on board, 3500 × 3500 mm (2 panels).
© 2003 Takashi Murakami/Kaikai Kiki Co., Ltd. All Rights Reserved.

Plate 6 George Herriman, *Krazy Kat*. Original ink and
coloured pencil drawing for the strip, undated.
Krazy Kat © King Features Syndicate.

The One

Who comes
To Quest-
ion
Him-
self

Has cared for mankind

Patchen

Plate 7 Kenneth Patchen, From *Hallelujah Anyway,* 1966. *Hallelujah Anyway* © 1966 by Kenneth Patchen. Used by permission of New Directions Publishing Corporation.

Plate 8 Alan Moore (writer), Stephen R. Bissette et al. (art), *Saga of the Swamp Thing* #22 (1984), p. 19. From 'Saga of the Swamp Thing' #22 © 1984 DC Comics. All Rights Reserved.

theory. The bear signifies, or actually is, a social relationship between creatures, but not one based on status or debt, which is attributed to the object as gift. This particular relationship is represented as really loving, in the same way that it may be with a companion animal or human friend. Layered within it is the history of inter-species relationships between biological humans and their companion animals (the small domestic animal or pet), as well as a complex, partly sentimental, partly anxious relationship to the wild as an exceptional biopolitical other to be mastered (the personable bear that yet does not talk, whose generic name is a graft from the modern politics of nature conservancy, manliness, and American imperialism bound up with the Roosevelt icon). Nilsen's bear lives for the man because of these social, political, and economic genes, and lives in the narrative as that problem creature – the natural-cultural web to which the man's love binds him – to which he must form his unique relationship.

That unique relationship is the renunciatory, exilic journey away from consumer production into the small planet wealth of an apparent waste land. Such a story, as in Cormac McCarthy's novel *The Crossing* (1994), can certainly end badly, both for the dog and the man. But in the beautiful, surprise ending to Nilsen's story, the man gives the cherished bear away to a child armed with an automatic rifle, and with whom he speaks without either one understanding the other's language (the child's is rendered in cursive scribbles). It is clear that the rifle is not causal here: when asked for the bear, the man looks silently at it for two panels, looks silently at the boy for one panel, then says 'alright' while handing him the bear in a subsequent panel.[7] His deliberation suggests that either he did not think the child would kill him, or that he considers whether he can live without the bear. In either case, this act of giving affirms the natural-cultural web that the man's companionship with the teddy bear represents – one that extends its sympathies beyond age, race, and language barriers. In a world of encounters with dead and living deer and dogs, English- and non–English-speaking humans, children and adults, foraging poor and oil company workers, the teddy bear is a kind of sympathetic virus, a creature that will carry in its genes a social relationship built out of habitat co-existence, rather than human exceptionalism and its modern empire of consumer wealth, scarcity, and abundance, as it journeys among others. When this value of the bear is fully realized, and is detached from its existence as kept property, the quest is complete and its narrative ends. The last panels of the story depict a pack of dogs waking and deciding to pursue and accompany the man; he is no longer the centre of his own story.

When a writer or comics creator abandons modernist renunciation entirely as a narrative structure, as a quest for an alternative economic understanding, such renunciation may also arise as a kind of willed adaptation to historical catastrophe, and to a narrative built around events cascading from a rupture rather than events enchained in a quest. Two novels with this structure, in both of which the rupture is a global war that imposes as much as it clears a space for new economies of scarcity and abundance, are Michael Ondaatje's historical fiction *The English Patient* (1992) and Margaret Atwood's future fiction *Oryx and Crake* (2003).

The experience of modern trench warfare stripped an unprecedented number of citizens of the European West to bare life of an unprecedented degree and scale, an exposure to an anxious or violent breakdown of human/inhuman distinctions, an exposure felt by non-combatants in the economic deprivations of a gargantuan military consumption, in the shadow of the airborne bomb, and in the horror of genocidal camps. A characteristic expression of this historical rupture turned to modernist individual renunciation is Robert Graves's *Goodbye to All That* (1929), which captured the disillusion of men in the First World War, as viewed by a British writer who chose the modernist expatriate life of removal to margins of Europe then considered socially and economically primitive – Majorca and Brittany. In Ondaatje's novel of the Second World War, his four principal characters also say goodbye to those societies that have embroiled them in their war work – as undercover military agents, as an army nurse, and as a sapper specializing in defusing bombs. Refusing to return home in the wake of German retreat, they inhabit the ruins of a deserted Italian villa. The shattered, partly inhospitable nature of the villa and the scarcity of food and necessities underlie a life lived with subsistence gardening and barter, with ingenious forms of leisure and play, and entirely without consumer wealth (a diminishing stock of morphine, emissary from another world and unavailable from cultivation or barter, is nearly an exception, the by-product of war machinery now salvageable by the nurse; it is a *pharmakon*, a medicine at once for forgetting and remembering that prompts the English patient's stories; and it is perhaps the ghost, in the novel, of the novel's own real-world economic life, a double-edged Pure Trance). The imposed scarcities of the villa, and the transient, Edenic enclosure of the life created there, mirror the North African desert and its oases of inhabitation that are at the centre of the English patient's story. In both the war-ravaged countryside and the nomadic desert, the novel's characters find in the absence of consumer production and wealth an alternative world of work, pleasures, and loves. The English patient speaks of his generation of desert explorers between the wars, of their love of the desert as an evidently modernist quest and renunciation for alternative values, selves, and words for them, in a waste land:

I came to hate nations. We are deformed by nation-states. Madox died because of nations.

The desert cannot be claimed or owned – it was a piece of cloth carried by the winds, never held down by stones, and given a hundred shifting names long before Canterbury existed, long before battles and treaties quilted Europe and the East ... All of us, even those with European homes and children in the distance, wished to remove the clothing of our countries. It was a place of faith. We disappeared into landscape.[8]

What has changed for the English patient, and for the others in the villa, is that the desert is no longer somewhere to travel to, a place of ascetic insulation from the material and ideological barrage of one's native society. It is now virtually everywhere in the wake of war; it is a destructive or erosive history tearing into lives that may never have thought to choose it or journey in search of it. When Ondaatje's characters refuse to leave the villa, it cannot be a refusal simply to return to normal life, but rather a refusal to return to rebuild normal life, and a decision to work otherwise. The burned patient is a post-human cipher for this violent yet creative rupture, this terrible beauty born. Like the desert, this problem creature resists any exclusive claims of family, nation, race, name; he is a story, a genealogy uncovered by the novel's ruptured narrative fabric. Our bodies and selves, says the English patient, are a kind of crossroads of natural history, technological habitats, and social worlds, of self and others, human and non-human:

> We die containing the richness of lovers and tribes, tastes we have swallowed, bodies we have plunged into and swum up as if rivers of wisdom, characters we have climbed into as if trees, fears we have hidden in as if caves. I wish for all this to be marked on my body when I am dead. I believe in such cartography – to be marked by nature, not just to label ourselves on a map like the names of rich men and women on buildings. We are communal histories, communal books. We are not monogamous in our taste or experience.[9]

Indeed, the English patient is a darkly burned shell, a blank face, a mere inky outline of a person of mysteriously plastic identity. What this shell has lost, ground peacock bone has helped replace.[10] He is an example of what I have suggested is manifest in the modern icon – and most remarkably in the invention of the cartoon figure in comics literature – an organic historicity that Michel Foucault argues overtakes the human sign as it loses its taxonomic stability in modern language and representation. He is similarly the icon of a habitat, or more precisely, of self and self-recognition that is inseparable from habitat production. At the novel's end, one character, the sapper, finds an alternative to his military work – his genius for turning the dark commodities of modern warfare into harmless refuse – in the medical profession, revealing his subtle absorption of the nurse and her work, 'containing the richness of lovers' in his new self. Of the nurse, we are denied a narrative of where she goes or what she does after the war. Although the final image of the novel suggests that she and the sapper remain embedded in each other, it is left for us to imagine what shapes this may take in her. A quest is teleological, but a rupture does not know closure, and can move in multiple directions.

There is a tradition of such transitional figures, problem creatures who straddle a fateful historical rupture between two bodily and economic lives, that reaches back at least as far as William Golding's *The Inheritors* (1955), a sombre novel that plunges the reader into a detailed prehistoric habitat bereft of consumer production or wealth, an exercise in radically different structures of feeling, in which the family members of a Paleolithic human species encounter a clan of early *Homo sapiens* who think them closer to devils or animals than to fellow humans. Although the family is demonized and nearly destroyed, its traces left for a future paleontology, its progeny is hesitantly assimilated into the tribe, not as pets but as children and future kin. Golding taps sophisticated variations on an historicist anxiety about the representation of human species that was initiated by Wells in *The Time Machine* and popularized by V.T. Hamlin's syndicated strip *Alley Oop* (from 1933). In *Alley Oop* we find a common primitivist fantasy of plenitude of vitality, purpose, and identity amidst conventional scarcity (prehistoric life). Here in the land of Moo, the unity of Hamlin's large, abstractly loopy, pleasing cartoon style for the strip converges with the unity of its liminally human (or not yet human) lives and habitat. In a sequence from 1946, Oop and a scientist from the future discuss the invasion of this habitat by a forerunner of modern civilized humanity, the Cro-Magnons, who are represented as 'ruthless,' more tediously businesslike creatures, if more intelligent (see fig. 3.2). Noteworthy in relation to the modernist fantasy embedded in style, however, is that the 'cro-mags' are not drawn in the usual strip/Moo style, but in

3.2 V.T. Hamlin, *Alley Oop*, 10–12 August 1946. Newspaper Enterprise Association. *Alley Oop*: © United Feature Syndicate, Inc.

a more mimetic realist manner, entirely free of caricature. This curious aesthetic strategy results both in a closer identification of the bad cro-mags with our twentieth-century selves, and in the opposite, a distancing from them as particular personalities (rather than abstract creaturely symbols like Oop), with whom we are more free to withhold readerly identification. The latter effect is one that Scott McCloud has recognized as peculiar to the aesthetics of comics, in which the greater the stylistic abstraction of character, the greater the ease of fantasy identification by individual readers, and the greater the mimetic realism, the greater the distance from a reader. While this cannot be a universal rule, it finds a powerful example here, in the disjunction of the two styles in one complex interaction of pre-human and human figures that represent competing ideas of wealth. For Hamlin as for Golding, there is a vision of historical descent into the human from some pre-human being, combined with a post-human fantasy identification with, perhaps even rebirth in, an alternative style of being.

The idea of evolutionary and social-historical rupture is also the basis of Pierre Boulle's *La Planète des singes* (1963), a novel best known for its immensely successful film adaptation, *Planet of the Apes* (1967), along with its sequels and remake. The problem creature who is an icon for this rupture appears more subtly in J.M. Coetzee's novel *Disgrace* (2000), where he is again, as in Ondaatje's novel, a burned man, here the victim of a longer war embedded in the fabric of South African social history. David Lurie begins as a handsome man with a comfortably bourgeois urban life; an improper sexual liaison and a dramatic turn of events leave him without work, on the country property of his daughter, where intruders set him on fire, burning away his hair and disfiguring his face and ear. The physical change echoes the novel's theme, the loss of face, experienced as exile from both worldly and inner stability. Though at the beginning of the novel Lurie is convinced that he is too old to change his ideas and values, after the affair and the burning, and in particular, as he works and lives among non-human animals, his sense of identity and the structures of feeling with which he relates to others, human and animal, black and white, male and female, yield to an unsuspected plasticity. Lurie sees himself and his daughter as a kind of passing species, and in the black farmer Petrus, their inheritor; the daughter's mixed-race child, like Golding's changeling, will inhabit a future beyond the ruptures of African modernity that is strictly unguessable. It is difficult to avoid the allegorical implications of the Jewish Lurie family as transitional figures in a discontinuous history whose future will unexpectedly be founded, like the Christian Church on its rock (Petrus), on beings their white society had once routinely animalized, as exceptions within and from the human.

This historical narrative and the problem creature at its fault line, thrust into a new comprehension of work, pleasure, and what Haraway calls companion species by an unlooked-for fate, finds its most explicit expression in Margaret Atwood's future fiction *Oryx and Crake* (2003), which circles back to Wells's *The Island of Dr. Moreau* for its end-of-millennium inspiration. Here the transitional figure, overcome by a catastrophic transformation in natural and social history instigated (but not successfully mastered) by a Moreau-like visionary scientist, is a man once named Jimmy, now known only as the Abominable Snowman to himself, and as Snowman to others – both symbols of ephemeral being. Following a biological holocaust, he may be the last *Homo sapiens* in existence. 'It's given Snowman a bitter pleasure to adopt this dubious label. The Abominable Snowman – existing and not existing, flickering at the edges of blizzards, apelike man or manlike ape, stealthy, elusive, known only through rumours and through its backward-pointing footprints.'[11] But Snowman does not live at the edges of his own human community, which has vanished. He lives at the edges of a community of genetically engineered humans, no longer *Homo sapiens* but something else, with cat-green eyes, who purr. These felinomorphic people live in a world partly awash with the material detritus of the Snowman's past society, and partly overgrown by a liberated natural fertility. They are presented as an Edenic people, as noble savages, but not a people Snowman can identify as his own. He lives with a sense of species extinction – or, more precisely, with a paradoxical sense that humanity can only survive its history in a shape not recognizably human. This is not only an alienating feeling. At the end of the novel, Snowman gazes at the sky before dawn: 'On the eastern horizon there's a greyish haze, lit now with a rosy, deadly glow. Strange how that colour still seems tender. He gazes at it with rapture; there is no other word for it. *Rapture*. The heart seized, carried away, as if by some large bird of prey.'[12] We can only escape our destructive history, Atwood seems to suggest, recalling Mizuno's *Pure Trance*, if we release our very identities and responsibilities to all that we regard as non-human nature, no matter how dangerous or benign with respect to our desires and needs. But here Atwood gently corrects Wells: the cat woman, not the fearful storyteller, is more likely to survive.

This futurological lesson, in which natural and social history converge in a catastrophic rupture and a plastic rapture of what it is to be human, and what may be its experience of wealth, is not restricted to narrative literature and comics. Atwood's message has a precedent in the gorgeous picture-poems produced by the bedridden Kenneth Patchen in the 1960s. Patchen is, apart from Marianne Moore, the other great bestiary poet of the modern century, in whose idiosyncratic work the problem creature and modern writing intersect, merge, and engender each other in an apocalyptic vision of historical rupture and animal futures. His picture-poems are painted (or occasionally silk-screened) images that include creatures, text, and ambiguous or non-figurative forms in fields of variegated texture and colour. Common to each picture-poem is an address to the reader, either explicitly in the text, or implicitly in the gaze of a creature or creatures. Both modes of hailing the reader are at work in 'My name is Dobble …' (1968), in which the spiky head of a creature with a long snout or beak and a huge eye emerges from the top of a decorated cylinder, beside which is written, 'MY NAME / IS DOBBLE / AND I / LIVE / IN A / USED / MILK / BOTTLE / What's / with you, / friend?' This picture-poem combines the estrangement effect of the creature's fellow recognition of us, with that of the creature's restrictive but delightfully recycled habitat. The same doubly estranging production of the human/ animal and its habitat seems to invite us into 'In Perkko's grotto …' (1966), in which two fantastic creatures, upright and quadruped, smile at us while we read: 'IN PERKKO'S / GROTTO / Everybody / gets along / Just fine / Why / Even / The best / champagne / Tastes like elderberry wine!'[13] The quadruped figure leads one to think of the 'grotto' as a wilderness cave, and its harmonious relations as the expression of a kind of Romantic animal primitivism. But the introduction of champagne leads one to revise the image of the grotto as something more like an urban club, perhaps one of the jazz clubs in which Patchen performed his poetry. In a final twist, the costly, status-soaked champagne that is a cliché of modern bourgeois wealth is valuable here only insofar as it measures up to a cliché of domestic or primitive, non-commodity manufacture, elderberry wine. What really tastes better? And to whose tastes? 'Who are you,' these picture-poems seem to ask, 'and where, how do you want to live?'

Such questions are not merely existential, in Patchen's iconographic poetry, but historical, driven by and embedded in an expression of the poet's social and historical moment as one of violence and possibility. Patchen was always an explicitly political poet, and his vision of the planet in the 1960s is conditioned by his commitment to the political and social struggles of the 1930s and the horrors of the Second World War, layered beneath the wars and injustices of the present. His poetry is designed to transfigure his readers and their relationship to this history; it is designed to be revolutionary. 'I believe that the revolutions of the future,' his avatar in The Journal of Albion Moonlight (1941) predicts, 'will be concerned with altering the minds of men, with vomiting out all that is insane for his animal.'[14] An inheritor of William Blake, Patchen works to elicit lyrical revelations of radically expanded human possibility, animal kinship and plasticity, and feelings of abundance from an epic vision of decadent history. What literary scholar Larry Smith sees in Patchen's earlier paratactic poems and drawings is even more true when the two are merged into a single iconic field akin to comics:

Like the illuminated pages of William Blake, the ancient Celts, or of the Bible, they are intended not merely to 'decorate' but to bring about the light of awareness. A highly intuitive, imaginative, and associational art, Patchen's work is based on the belief that a freely created form will deliver a creative response and will thus free the viewer's mind ... Such an engaged text demands the audience's working out the relationships of the two forms, a relationship characterized not by logic, but by free and imaginative associations. One must surrender to the wonder of the synthesis and thus be transformed through the very act of perception.[15]

In other words, these picture-poems are intended to spark in the reader a new creative vision of self and historical habitat alike, human and animal, animate and inanimate, mundane and fantastic, that will root the production of self in a habitat production that demands co-existence and recognition between unlike creatures, unexpected companion species. 'The One / Who comes / To / Quest – / ion / Him – / self / Has cared for mankind,' reads the text of another picture-poem (see colour plate 7). The words are presented by two (not 'one') fantastic creatures, one humanoid, the other avian, neither clearly gendered. The words 'The One' are suspended in cool, blue isolation from the rest of the text in the upper right corner of a predominantly warm, yellow-red painting bursting with seeds and branches of colour. The self as one, as singularity, and as male, is here an icon of abstraction itself, an icon that is visually and literally questioned – and with the reader hailed – by problem creatures who claim kinship. The self 'who comes' to that question, who falls into that historical crevasse of a modernity fed by war, will feel new sympathies or responsibilities, will have 'cared for mankind,' the uncertain species of the 'one' grasped as a question.

In most of his work, Patchen's historical vision is open-ended yet sensually lavish, but the cinder-skinned people of 'An interview with THE FLOATING MAN' and the lurking creatures in 'Come now, my child' reveal that such a post-human world might just as well be catastrophic (and fatal) as it may be utopian (and hoped for), the object of dreams and quest as of blindness and destruction. This careful inclusiveness, in which wonder and estrangement coexist in profound reciprocity, finds compelling icons in a picture-poem having the text 'What the story tells itself / when there's nobody around / to hear it' written across the top of a spare representation of two figures, the one hardly more than an ambiguous, ghostly outline with two black eyes, extending a limb across the other, a fishlike figure ornamented with a flower, amid some jagged black shapes.[16] The 'story,' whether understood as art or as history, is the only recognizably human trace in the picture, the trace of a romance not or no longer human (or is it?). This narrative voice, its modest pleasure, its becalmed emptiness, its steady returning of our gaze: is it there, who we want, what we need? Patchen grasps the human as a narrative rather than an identity, the production of an event. His creatures, marooned among a mere handful of words and scattered objects, enjoy what wealth? They mean to produce in us a pleasure of creaturely encounter (self and other) that does not arise out of the dialectic of modern consumer scarcity and satisfaction; these new abundances of contact and mutation are made possible as we invent companionships, imagine cohabitation with them.

Patchen's work is evidently indebted to William Blake; but there is just as evidently a debt that is not literary, and which belongs to an iconographic bestiary that Blake did not provide. In concluding this chapter, I will return to the comics genre touched upon in my discussion of *Dogs and Water*, and attempt to sketch out that graphic novel's wider context amid the overwhelming, contemporary multitude of problem creatures caught up in similarly re-imagined modern histories. In comics, these dramas of post-human adaptation or catastrophic evolution are played out again and again with the iconological force of a mystery play.

Batman and Spider-Man are only the most famous of a host of animal-human hybrids in comics since the late 1930s, all of which express fantasies of isolation and violent mastery over any creature that would contaminate the good of their urban environments. These animalized superheroes, along with their technologically or alien-infected cousins, are post-human kin to the other principal figures of comics history, the so-called 'funny animals' of James Swinnerton's pioneering *Little Bears* (1895) and *Mount Ararat* (1901), Pat Sullivan and Otto Messmer's *Felix the Cat* (1923), Walt Disney's *Mickey Mouse* (1930) and *Donald Duck* (1934), Walt Kelly's *Pogo* (1943), Tove Jansson's *Moomin* (1954), Robert Crumb's *Fritz the Cat* (1959), and countless kindred in other comic strips. This genealogy stretches even further to include those in animation and puppetry for film and television, such as Chase Craig's Porky Pig (1943) and other Looney Tunes figures, or Jim Henson's Muppets, and those in illustrated books, from Beatrix Potter's *Peter Rabbit* (1901) to Jean de Brunhoff's *Babar* (1931), through to their myriad descendants in children's books, toys, games, and television today.

The significance of these figures' emergence in largely segregated children's and youth genres will be considered in the next chapter. Here I will focus on genre and art comics in which problem creatures embody a critical relationship at once to modernity and to the human. A starting point is Grant Morrison's Animal Man, the superhero he reinvented for DC Comics in the 'Deus Ex Machina' episodes of 1989–90. Animal Man can embody any attribute of any animal at any time – a kind of ultimately plastic composite of single-species hybrids like The Wasp or Wolverine. Almost too powerful to make the average villain plot interesting, Animal Man becomes in Morrison's hands the centre of a metafictional exploration of human identity and history. Wandering through the weird iconological landscapes of genre comics itself, Animal Man seeks to reverse the violence and death that has marred his own life/story. In the end, he confronts the figure of Morrison himself, who reveals that Animal Man, along with his narrative, is a confused by-product of his own author's grief over the death of his cat, Jarmara, and his commitment to Animal Rights activism. Animal Man learns a familiar environmentalist lesson, that nature (like the iconographic world of comics) is a web of connected and interdependent creatures, and that his identity cannot be abstracted from it (nor from the world of comics). In other words, genre comics narratives repress their own non-anthropocentric premises, just as modern histories do. It is a double lesson that only a genre story that turns the cosmic rupture of a superhero's acquisition of power into one of his loss of sense of abundance, of worth, can reveal. Yet, at the heart of this lesson is the limit to plasticity in any way that can be valued in word or icon: the extinction of individual selves and species that cannot be wished away by *any* imagination of power or plenty.

Morrison's *Animal Man* appeared several years after Alan Moore's *Saga of the Swamp Thing* (1984), which offered a more literalized representation of the human embedded in non-human nature (here, of human in vegetable nature). But this fantasy is more clearly one of catastrophic adaptive evolution: in his origin story of the monstrous Swamp Thing, Moore imagines a man, Alec Holland, decomposing in a swamp after being bombed, while plant life ingests his disintegrated particles and becomes 'infected' by a 'consciousness that does not realize it is no longer alive.' Moore tells us that it is wrong to think that the resulting new growth, 'the swamp thing[,] was Alec Holland, somehow transformed into a plant.' Rather, 'it was a plant that thought it was Alec Holland.'[17] The problem creature ultimately rejects this spectral human identity while retaining its heritage of human knowledge, feeling, and bodily form (see colour plate 8). Driven to a marginal, shadowy habitat by modern industrial and urban development, the Swamp Thing is thus paradoxically both a reflection of non-human nature that is subject to human violence or waste, and a fantasy of human nature that might escape the oppressive, anthropocentric identity of the human as such. Such iconic deformations and re-imaginings of human identity – in a confrontation with modern violence emblemized by extinction – similarly inform, in very different ways, the future-fiction genre comic by Brian Vaughan, *Y: The Last Man* (2002), and the renowned historical-fiction and memoir comic by Art Spiegelman, *Maus* (1980). Between the iconology of *Maus* and of Patchen's work lies the gulf between a modern habitat that has been, and what it can be.

Chapter Four

Growing Wonder

On first consideration, those I have called *problem creatures* might seem to dwell only in the margins of the great tradition of modern literature – as principal figures in comics and other non-canonical forms and genres, or as subsidiary elements in canonical texts. While I and other writers do strive to shed light on the unsuspected number of non-human creatures scurrying beneath the floorboards of this canonical literary tradition, and to give greater significance to their sightings, it is also true that for Western readers such creatures have always already played a principal role in the bright light of day, and today ubiquitously so, it seems without our wanting to acknowledge it.

From the turn of the twentieth century right up to the present time in the West, our introduction to reading and to the experience of literature itself has been dominated by and mediated by a menagerie of talking animals and other non-human creatures, from Winnie-the-Pooh, Babar the Elephant and Curious George, to Aslan the Lion, Wilbur the Pig, and Teenage Mutant Ninja Turtles; to Big Bird and Reader Rabbit; and many, many more, today surrounded by commodity avatars in movies, stuffed toys, games, and foods. Whether in school or in the home, we routinely don an animal mask in order to introduce those strange things, books and learning, to our children.[1] In this chapter, I will argue not only that the mask remains on the wearer, but also that this curious, overlooked dimension of modernist primitivism is the proper end of modernism itself, in which a once elitist appreciation of the difficult merges with a postmodern commitment to the accessible.

Quite apart from literary situations, the special relationship between children and other living species is a growing area of interest in psychology and social sciences. The most influential study of this habitat relationship remains Gene Myers's *Children and Animals* (1998), which foregrounds the centrality of animals in many children's lives and studies pre-verbal social and linguistic development between them. Myers's starting point is the sense of wonder that often arrests the attention of a young child interacting with animals. This wonder is the foundation of a primal social experience, that of 'somehow recognizing and [being] captivated by the nearly ineffable sameness-and-difference of another living animal.' Children recognize both continuity and connections with other species, and differences from them, and thus understand themselves as embedded in an 'ecology of subjects' among species.[2] This recognition and wonder appears to be universal, since companion animals, especially for children, are evidenced in the most diverse cultures through history and around the world.[3] Across oral heritages that would include both children and adults in their audiences, whether the tales are secular (e.g., the fairy tale) or sacred (e.g., totemic), relationships between humans and animals are central, often representing transformations between species that prefigure the plasticity of modernity's animal icons. With the invention of print and, at the same time, of printed illustration, the child's special relationship to animals finds a striking documentary record – one curiously entwined with reading and writing.

From the fifteenth to the eighteenth century, the official line regarding other species, as inferior existences contrasted with the educated or educable human, remained as the Anglo-Saxon Aelfric had expressed it in his *Colloquy* (c. 1000), one of the earliest texts written for children: 'MASTER: I ask you, why are you learning so diligently? PUPIL: Because we do not wish to be as stupid animals, who know nothing except grass and water.'[4]

For over two hundred years, the book industry avoided folk traditions and their animal creatures as heretical, with the signal exception of Aesop's fables. Yet the fables, along with a large body of romances which thrived on animal magic, were produced during this time for adults, who likely read them aloud to diverse illiterate listeners, including children (for example, the sketch of a cross-class, cross-generational audience in Cervantes' *Don Quixote* [1605]).[5] The rise of printed literature for children during this time was restricted to language primers and books of morals and manners. At the beginning of the eighteenth century, this tradition took a turn. Children began to be directly addressed with books designed to engage them with illustrations from their own everyday life; indeed, such artwork became the norm for the new genre, and animals are by far its most common subject.[6] For the first time, books written in English directly registered a human life, considered actual rather than supernatural, pervaded by a recognition of other species in its habitat. At the same time, fantasy creatures suddenly abounded. The romance literature discussed above began to be printed in inexpensive illustrated chapbook editions, becoming 'the "underground" or "comic" literature of their age.'[7] Jonathan Swift's *Gulliver's Travels* (1726), among other contemporary literary works, also underwent this transformation, destined for a crossover child-adult audience. Finally, English-speaking readers were seduced by the immensely influential folk tales that were a popular print genre in France; it was the age of Charles Perrault's fairy tales (1697; first English translation, 1729), which gave birth to that icon of human-animal storytelling, Mother Goose, and to stories now completely assimilated into English tradition, such as 'Cinderella' and 'Red Riding Hood.'

One of Perrault's tales, 'Puss-in-Boots,' offers an historical forerunner of the modern problem creature in the icon of a talking cat who represents a kind of pivot in human possibility between inherited social identity and wealth and a strictly bourgeois notion of the self-made man. The cat is left as property to the third and youngest, otherwise destitute son of a deceased miller. Before the boy can use the animal merely for meat and fur, the cat speaks up, saying that he represents an unexpected bounty. The cat proceeds by trickery to generate the wealth and title of a feudal lord for the boy, and marriage to the daughter of a king. The moral appended by Perrault is: 'It's all very well to be born rich, / And pass on wealth from father to son; / But hard work, know-how, and quick wits / Are just as useful, when you're young.' Here, the new self-made man of Enlightenment bourgeois ideology is a hybrid animal-man, not a regression but a prototype, something the human may potentially become. Nor is the animal figure an accident of fantasy. The boy uses his childhood knowledge of the animal, the fruit of his idle wonder, to judge its worth to him: 'Although the cat's master did not set any great store by what the cat said, he had seen this cat perform some amazing acrobatic feats in order to catch rats and mice, as for example when he hung from his feet or hid in the flour and played dead, and so he was quite hopeful that the cat could help him in his dire straits.' [8] The gentle irony here, that the cat's ability to talk is less remarkable to the boy than are its other signs of cleverness and craft, points to the kind of recognition of and attention to the different-and-same subjectivity of other species that Myers finds in children today. The boy's skill in 'reading' this other animal, and his co-dependence on it for his – and the cat's, who has also been dispossessed by the miller's family – rise to wealth, is an ecological lesson that underlies the historical one. In 'Puss-in-Boots,' the wealth appropriated from an obsolescent feudal aristocracy is won by a liberal individual not freed of kinship restrictions, but bound to new ones with other species.

An 'ecology of subjects' which associates children and language acquisition with a non-anthropocentric habitat is not only symptomatically readable in this early literary tradition; it emerges as a subject in its own right in literature of this period. Along with a new genre of talking animal biography, there is a wider appeal to a non-human perspective of human-animal worlds. An exemplary instance is the tale of 'Old Zig-Zag' (c. 1766) by the pioneer of children's writing and publishing,

John Newbery, in which the protagonist has a magical horn allowing him to understand the languages of animals around him. But Zig-Zag is so horrified by the amount of abuse he learns is inflicted upon these co-habiting species that he concludes that 'man, proud, imperious, cruel man, is the most unjust of the animals,' and 'either burnt his horn, or gave it to Mr. Newbery, who daily employs it in writing the conversation of birds, beasts and other animals.'[9] The didactic literature of an ecology of subjects is a very long way from the instructions of Aelfric. What does it mean to come to literature, and increasingly to writing itself, by listening to such voices, and gazing at their faces and forms, printed on the page?

Myers's work suggests an intriguing answer, which reaches deep into our understanding of modern literature and its current turning points. In his study of interactive relationships between young children and animals, Myers argues that children recognize patterns of behaviour in animals (human and non-human) that constitute a set of pre-verbal meanings regarding all social others. These are patterns of individual agency, coherence, affect, and continuity, which constitute the other animal as another socially constituted subjectivity, another self, for the child. Even as adults, we carry around this core set of non-verbal patterns as symbols that allow us to identify ourselves and others as co-inhabitants of an ecology of subjects. This does not mean that children simply identify with animals indiscriminately; while they may project anthropomorphic meanings upon them, they do not do so without a persistent sensitivity to and wonder at both similarity and difference among humans and other species, interactions with which they are physically and linguistically experimenting. In playing with or merely watching a classroom pet, for example, a child recognizes a common subjectivity in its pre-verbal patterns of behaviour, and both similarity and difference in its modes of expression and interaction. In other words, the child learns to distinguish its individual and human self from other selves by reading animal behaviour, both human and non-human, via patterns as symbolic forms. Myers distinguishes symbolic from verbal language, because instead of being founded on conventional or arbitrary signs, the animate symbol partakes of both indexical meaning (from material contiguity, as smoke is a sign of fire) and iconic meaning (from shared qualities or similitude, as a portrait is a sign of a sitter). This does not mean that human-animal relations are not conventional, or that the conventions of other species need not be learned, but that all such interaction is layered on a symbolic recognition of inter-subjectivity that rests on indexical and iconic patterns of similitude and difference, a symbolic recognition whose language is generated as the growing person affirms, and tests the limits of, the possibility for self-other communication in a habitat.

Myers observes that 'symbols stemming from this core commonality constitute a special category of animal symbols, ones with great subjective relevance.'[10] This language category is not limited to its somatic basis or to children's art. As we have seen in the brief historical survey above, the fascination with animal-human recognition and inter-species subjective relations has always pushed its iconic languages into children's language learning and literature. It is also one of the strongest traditions in the art of comics, a crossover art that has always rooted itself in a children's and youth audience, which precisely merges verbal writing with iconography, so that the image is expressed as a pictographic line while the word is expressed as a visual figure, and which has released into the past century a flood of problem creatures demanding recognition in our literature, just as now, our ecological awareness has required that other and new species gain recognition in our habitats. It is tempting to believe that the language of comics – and its extension in cinematic animation – has achieved such growing importance in recent years because of its unique ability to render the languages of this ecology of subjects in its plastic, iconographic line. Comics, like children's literature, may long have been considered too simple to merit literary scholarship – not *difficult* enough in their verbal or visual craft, as a modernist might judge it, to allow for refined interpretations, hence for the development of the humanist citizen, who is a refined

reader of the world around her, around him. But this view has
been blind to the iconographic languages that have created
profoundly significant problem creatures in the verbal and
illustrated characterology of children's literature, and in the
iconic figures and environments of comics, alike. These creatures and habitats, though stigmatized as childish, are in their
uncanny or experimental wandering at the borders of human
identity and happiness, among the most important expressions
of modern life and its often contradictory or conflicted assumptions about selfhood, kinship, and wealth. And they are, like
the stigma itself, ironically not so easy to read. Pushing at the
very definitions of writing and of humanist education, they are
in every modernist sense, difficult. On our small planet, with
its growing industrialization for consumer production and jos-
tling populations, this writing on the wall is imperative to learn
and to teach.

   In the remainder of this chapter, I will discuss specific works
of literature and comics for children or youths, from modernist to contemporary periods, for their diverse expressions of a
modern ecology of subjects and wealth. A survey of these vast
areas cannot be attempted here, not even of the most canonical
works, but I will discuss some of the latter, along with those
lesser known, that have elicited the strongest sense of my own
wonder.

   The attempt to create stories of non-human animals, not only
with animal perspectives but also with whole animal worlds
largely independent from human life and alternative to them in
culture and economy, begins to flourish at the end of the nineteenth century with Rudyard Kipling's fanciful *Jungle Books*
(1894–5) and the Canadian naturalist and writer E.T. Seton's
Wild Animals I Have Known (1898). It was in this decade that
realism came to animal fiction. The *Jungle Books* were unique,
M.F. Thwaite has observed, for 'blend[ing] realism and the
fable in a new and startling way' and giving birth to a new kind
of problem creature.[11] Inspired by Indian folklore, Buddhist
scriptures, and by a primitivist anthropology that renders animal cultures as similar to human tribal cultures (a modern tra-

dition reaching forward to Barbara Gowdy's powerful novel of elephant life, *The White Bone* [1998]), Kipling creates in the child Mowgli the iconic figure of a human that is acculturated to the alternative habitat and psychological life of another species, and recognizes this duality as existentially profound, exposing the uncertainty of the human-animal divide. 'I am two Mowgli's,' he sings, while laughing and crying, as 'two things fight together in me as the snakes fight in the spring,' and 'my heart is heavy with the things that I do not understand.'[12] And in a subtle sense, both the jungle and the village, between which Mowgli is torn, are themselves fusions of conventional human and animal representations. The village is a non-Western tribal society that most of Kipling's readers, if not the author himself, would have considered less civilized and closer to animal life than Kipling's own. Conversely, the jungle is highly structured by anthropomorphic cultures and languages among species. Hence, while Mowgli is a figure of primitivist asceticism, finding greater satisfaction in Kipling's fantasy of the wealth of feral life, social and material, than in human civilization, he is also a figure of ascetic aporia, of reduction to an animal identity and habitat economy that have no existing terms, and which he must now invent, in order to thrive. Similar to Moreau's South Pacific island, Kipling's exotic alternative world fuses species and habitat difference – naturalist aspects of what he calls the Law of the Jungle – with cultural discourses and texts drawn from Kipling's colonialist experience of South Asia, in order to generate a new icon of the modern individual, one who must re-invent his self-recognition as a species in order to go about mere sustenance and welfare.

The realist register of the modern animal story is exemplified in the rise of naturalist animal writing during the 1890s, such as Seton's, and it plays a minor though significant role in the vast menagerie of animal representation from then to the present day. Of course, all animal fiction depends on some measure of anthropomorphic fantasy. To speak of its realism is to measure its conformity to knowledge of other species provided either by natural science or by common experience. This measure

may be large or small, and still convey valuable challenges to
the imagination of how humans should live among other animals in their shared worlds. Realist representation of different
species' lives in art and literature is significant insofar as these
differences combine with others to articulate an alternative life
world for readers to inhabit as they identify with the problem
creatures generated therein, and to mark that world as a possible or plausible one for such identification, rather than as mere
fantasy. But the realist-fantasy distinction is not always obvi-
ous. In his discussion of anthropomorphism in Japanese *animé*,
Fred Patten describes the adaptation of Seton's *Bannertail: The
Story of a Gray Squirrel* (1922) into a cartoon television serial
(1979):

> The serial anthropomorphized Seton's naturalistic portrayal of
> Eastern North American forest animals to the point of putting
> them in clothing, situating them in a small animal village, and
> even letting them quote Shakespeare. But one incident in Seton's
> story, which was expanded into a full episode ... featured Banner
> innocently eating a hallucinogenic mushroom and psychedeli-
> cally freaking out. Early *animé* fans promptly added this to their
> examples of 'You'll never believe what they air in Japan on TV
> cartoons!'[13]

Even in such strong fantasy genres as are found in manga and
animé, a realist register may be crucial. In Hayao Miyazaki's
film *Princess Mononoke* (1997), which is permeated by magic
and supernatural beings and set in a pre-modern historical
period, the realist depiction of ways of life of forest animals
is part of what is required to understand the narrative conflict
between human and animal interests as an ecological one, and
the problems of identity and justice that emerge in its contested
habitat as typical of actual and contemporary modern environments. This kind of partial realism is typical of animal lives in
literature and popular culture after the Victorian age, in which
the urge to create new kinds of creatures with strange ways of
inhabiting, producing, and reproducing their world – from the

silly to the sublime, from Mickey Mouse to St Mawr – overwhelms an austerely naturalistic representation.

A striking example of the ambivalence of the modern animal figure as this kind of problem creature is found in C.S. Lewis's immensely popular *Chronicles of Narnia* (1950–6). In the first published volume, *The Lion, The Witch and the Wardrobe* (1950), Lewis imagined a world in which animals talk, feel, and think very much like humans. More than that, Lewis imagined the god of this world – and, as we learn later in the series, of our world and the cosmos itself – in the form of a lion, named Aslan. The lion is frightening to the children protagonists of the novel, but also sensuously attractive, and pleasurably comforting when held or touched, just like a furry pet. With this device, Lewis created a potent metaphor for the awe-inspiring otherness and magnetic love and pleasure of his Christian God. But he did so by collapsing the Great Chain of Being, and finding in the physical, feral beast, conventionally a symbol of that unreal, corrupt part of human being that will be extinguished by the apocalyptic revelation of true Life, a symbol of its metaphysical and virtuous opposite. This is the radical edge in Lewis's fantasy: the vision of a partly human, partly non-human world ruled by the love and power of an ambiguous, ethically superior, and insistently sensual animal, in which the forging of an ecology of subjects among species is explicitly required by the romance plot. In this, Aslan and St Mawr are kindred beings. Yet Lewis may well have felt uncomfortable about this radical gesture, despite its platonic justification as a version of courtly love, for in subsequent volumes he takes pains to reinstate a chain of being that separates talking animals from conventional ones – frequently condemning the latter, as does the horse Bree in *The Horse and His Boy* (1954), as 'dumb and witless.' At the apocalyptic conclusion to *The Last Battle* (1956), all humanoid creatures and talking animals come before Aslan for final judgment before passing into either a paradisal afterlife or the shadow of oblivion. Not only are common animals excluded from this procession, but even those talking animals who fail to pass into paradise are turned into ordinary animals before

entering the darkness. Thus Lewis evokes the animal – its wonder and seduction – as well as the child – his or her difference
from adult ways of thinking – to work to produce the analogue
of a religious experience that ultimately demands the transcendence and extinction of both. He is so good at it, however,
that I doubt many of his readers have been willing to leave the
world of the animal and the child, thus powerfully created, to
the shadow world of mere metaphor, of signs to be left behind
as waste material in the production of a spiritual – and in his
second book, *Prince Caspian* (1951), deliberately meat-eating –
maturity.[14] The resulting tension between an ecology of subjects
and anthropocentric sovereignty, between human welfare and
its animal supplement, gives Narnia its abiding fascination. As
problem creatures ourselves, we may be drawn to Narnia more
deeply as an analogue of our modern habitat, and to its lion
Aslan for expressing the feeling of a real ecology of subjects,
both normally repressed, than to the human relationships to
divinity we are meant entirely to exchange them for.

Such an exchange is, however, absent from or tangential to
many children's modern texts that evoke an ecology of subjects among animals for their young listeners and readers. Such
is the world of the River and its hinterlands in Kenneth Grahame's *The Wind in the Willows* (1908), or of the Forest in Grahame's admirer's, A.A. Milne's, *Winnie-the-Pooh* (1926). Milne's
work is extraordinary for adopting the hybrid human-animal
characters of Grahame's novel – and of funny animal comics in the popular press (especially Mary Tourtel's straitlaced
Rupert Bear, who debuted in 1920) – and cultivating them in
the midst of self-reflexive narrative and wordplay which dis-
solve and recombine not only human-animal distinctions but
those between natural and artificial life. What are Pooh and his
stuffed and stitched friends, after all, but peaceful relatives of
Dr Moreau's sutured creations? No doubt, the House of Pain,
in which all life in Moreau's and our modernity must dwell,
expresses a truth about violence and suffering – inevitable to
welfare and essential to habitat, where lives feed on each other
– that is completely eclipsed in Milne's idyllic world. Those

who have grown up imaginatively in this world, as I have, will remember its idleness and indirection, its unhurried, solvent plots, with great fondness. Indeed, in Milne the affect of boredom finds its first devotional poet, who drains from it the gloomy dissatisfactions of the ennuyé Victorian, replacing the agonized restlessness of the individual consumer of life with an erratic responsiveness to nothing immediately signifying, the giddy boredom of the open. In Pooh, the perennial problem of 'what to do' is turned upside down: experiencing the problem itself is seductive as a state of being, as an always fertile ground, in mere sensibility to ambience, in pleasant reverie, or in the chatter of nonsense rhyme, for the beginnings, turnings, or returnings of actual plots and events. To be sure, this world shares in a common liberal dream of creative autonomy, and of life free of labour and suffering, that is displaced upon the child and the animal (and with curious self-reflexive resonances, upon the toy). But Milne's dream, in its articulation of an ecology of subjects that dislocates language from meaning, is also counter-productive to modern consumer wealth and scarcity.

The first of the Pooh stories begins with the sentence: 'Here is Edward Bear, coming downstairs now, bump, bump, bump, on the back of his head, behind Christopher Robin.' On the facing page is Ernest Shepard's illustration of this very scene, the small boy looking down at each step, dragging the teddy bear behind him, on its back and head first, holding one of its paws. Should one say the bear is looking up at the boy, or at the ceiling, or into space? The bear is little more than an outline – an oval form with sausage-shaped legs and arms, lines that indicate the limbs stitched to the body, and a few extra lines barely suggesting fur or shading. The head is simply a round form with a black spot for an eye, U-shapes for ears, and similar stitching lines. This and the drawing at the end of the chapter, in which Pooh sits on the edge of Christopher Robin's bathtub, are the only ones in which he appears inanimate, a lifeless toy, an 'it.' The storyteller continues: 'It is, as far as he knows, the only way of coming downstairs, but sometimes he feels that there really is another way, if only he could stop bumping for a moment and think of it. And then he feels that perhaps there isn't.'[15] So Pooh is endowed with life, with deliberative thought and personality. He is then renamed Winnie-the-Pooh. But before coming to this naming, it is worth noticing the curious effect of the introduction, which plays at creating a life that is avowedly both that of the stuffed animal and that of an imagined personality, and will soon cross over between the worlds of the family house, shared by the boy and the storyteller, and the forest shared by the boy and the toy animals. Pooh is invented as a companion personality – magically, both a familiar kind of manufactured product and a novel species of living creature. The cartoon simplicity of Pooh's face, an outline with dots for eyes, approaches the iconic simplicity of a toy, and makes no effort to render an actual or individual bear (or even, perhaps, a realist, individual toy bear). Pooh is, in fact, explicitly presented by illustrator and storyteller as iconic, as the graphic icon of a manufactured icon of an anthropomorphic animal (the teddy bear), and hence as a face that must be recognized as other, as a mere thing, before it is endowed with a specific nature, the life of a character. We are confronted with the question of its face, in other words, before we are invited to relate to it.

To appreciate the significance of this imaginative disruption, one only need consider the weight of the exchange reported by Derrida when philosopher Emmanuel Levinas is questioned by the eco-scholar John Llewellyn. Regarding Levinas's elaboration of an ethics founded on face-to-face recognition, Llewellyn asked a series of questions, including: 'Does the fact of having a face imply an aptitude for language? Does the animal have a face? Can one read "Thou shalt not kill" in the eyes of the animal?' These questions are essential to the question of whether any non-human animal may be recognized as an ethical subject, as opposed to a mere object for human ethics. Levinas purportedly answered: 'I cannot say at what moment you have the right to be called "face." The human face is completely different and only afterwards do we discover the face of an animal. I don't know if a snake has a face. I can't answer that question. A more specific analysis is needed.'[16] Derrida rightly observes that

Levinas insists on the exceptionality and primacy of the human face, while at the same time admitting to being unable to distinguish it from a non-human face. For Derrida, this undermines Levinas's anthropomorphic definition of ethics, and opens the question of whether the animal may be recognized as a companion subject in our world, another 'I.' Moreover, referring back to the psychological studies discussed earlier, it should appear unjustifiably hasty to claim that in childhood development, human faces are recognized in an evidently more immediate way than are non-human animal faces. The question of the animal face – whether we recognize a face at all – is key to the notion of an ecology of subjects. In most literature, any confrontation with this question is mediated by verbal language. In comics and picture books, it is more powerfully mediated by an iconology of the face that collapses the distance between existential perception (Levinas) and written sign (Derrida). What Derrida finds so poorly represented in philosophical writing is inscribed everywhere in modern children's literature.[17]

Pooh's face is easily read, what we might call *accessible*, yet it is also mysterious, once we force ourselves to ask what is actually there to be read, what kind of 'I.' Absurd as it seems, Pooh can hardly be less *difficult* than is Conrad's Lord Jim to pin down – like Jim's friend Stein's butterflies – to a species of person: is Pooh *one of us*, or is he something else we wish we were, or wish we lived with? I will suggest that Pooh's accessibility is not conventional, as a typical modernist reading would have it – that is, not the kind of conventionality that straitjackets modern society and imposes its tepid clichés of sentiment and thought with a quiet violence, which must be opposed by an avant-garde. Rather, Pooh's kind of accessibility is itself conventionally repressed. For it is a fact that we do not nearly understand why we recognize faces, nor how. Pooh's accessibility is a mystery, and when exposed in the play of Milne's and Shepard's signs, this accessibility is itself difficult – as I suggested earlier, a dislocation of language into surprising meaning. This is a difficulty that reaches to the heart of our recognition of an ecology of subjects and representation of habitat – at once of and beyond the human. Myers's work on pre-verbal signs of subject recognition, discussed earlier, suggests that this recognition may be based on an initial wonder before the icon – that Pooh, though graphic rather than living, evokes the full drama of subject recognition, as the reader confronts at first an undecidable figure, a thing, then with the textual construction of coherence, agency, affect, and continuity, is taught to identify the problem creature as an unexpected kind of animal – signally, as an example of a friend, a species of companion.

In Shepard's illustrations, Christopher Robin's face is similar in style to that of Pooh, a sketchy outline, with highly simplified, cartoon-stylized features. When I was a child, the hair, clothes, and face – and one-half of the name – signified to me as female. Despite the insistence of the male pronoun also supplied by Milne, nothing could convince me that Christopher Robin was not somehow both male and female, or neither, existing in some gender otherworld. This figure's forest existence (for me, his reality, since in the storyteller's world the animals were nearly absent), which was without human family, underscored this possibility. Christopher Robin is attractive as a child that is not anthropocentrically human, but human in some *sui generis*, forest-dependent way. One can imagine Pooh, Piglet, et al., in the forest without him, but not he in the forest without them. Who, or what, is he? The final illustration of the book is significant, a kind of mirror image of the first: Christopher Robin walking back upstairs, his face hidden, Pooh again upside-down and backwards, his face aimed either vacantly towards a wall or, if ascribed with personality, gazing towards the reader (see fig. 4.1). The landing is now visible at the top of the stairs, where a jumble of other stuffed animals awaits them, unseen in the initial illustration; one of them looks directly at Christopher Robin. Pooh's face now looks us in the eye, while the human boy's face demands that we imagine for ourselves what is not there to be seen. To appreciate the modernity of this representation, one only need compare Foucault's reading of the mirroring gazes of *Las Meninas*, Diego Velázquez's painting of 1656, which dramatizes the invisible construction of an

4.1 E.H. Shepard, page 146 of A.A. Milne's *Winnie-the-Pooh* (1926).
© The Estate of E.H. Shepard. From *Winnie-the-Pooh* by A.A. Milne,
illustrated by E.H. Shepard, copyright 1926 by E.P. Dutton, renewed
1954 by A.A. Milne. Used by permission of Dutton Children's Books,
A Division of Penguin Young Readers Group. All rights reserved.

exceptional sovereignty of spectator and painter, speaker and listener, writer and reader, who are supposed as human subjects to transcend the mundane worlds of nature and language. In *Las Meninas*, Foucault notes in passing that only the dog has no gaze, is a mere object.[18] By contrast, in Shepard's drawings the mirroring gazes of animals and person, the hiddenness of the person's face, the oscillation between mere objecthood and subjectivity in the animal figures as toys or persons, and the unification of cartoon style rather than of mimetic realism, draw the spectator and reader into a drama of representation that lacks such sovereignty, and reinforces the more open-ended process of learning a new subjective relationship amidst iconographic and verbal play.

I may now return to the matter of Pooh's name, which is offered like his face as a diverting problem for the reader. Despite Pooh's introduction as Edward Bear (one must speculate whether this is a generic British variation on the American Teddy, an actual British manufacturer's label, or simply an earlier name given in the storyteller's family), he is reintroduced with a name supplied by Christopher Robin: Winnie-the-Pooh. Passing over this discrepancy in names without comment, the storyteller is concerned with other problems: the apparently wrong gender of the name (should not Winnie be female?) and its unusualness (the tripartite form, and the word 'Pooh,' which is given alternative explanations at the end of the first chapter and in the author's Introduction). But these are swept aside, affirming the arbitrariness of signs and an individual power to name that is unconventional, even if it therefore turns to nonsense. This Saussurian lesson is underscored when the storyteller begins:

> Once upon a time, a very long time ago now, about last Friday, Winnie-the-Pooh lived in a forest all by himself under the name of Sanders.
> (*'What does 'under the name' mean?' asked Christopher Robin.*
> *'It means he had the name over the door in gold letters and lived under it'* ...)

The illustration on the facing page portrays Pooh sitting on a log, his back to a cave with a wood-framed doorway. Above the door is a sign in crude orthography with two backwards letters, 'MR. SANDERS,' beside a doorbell with the sign 'RNIG ALSO.'[19] The provenance of this name remains a mystery, but is indisputably Pooh's property, an assimilation to his home. Pooh is seated before a fire, gazing up at a trail of smoke risen in the air. The human elements of manufacture, and his posture and meditative aspect, allow us to identify with him as similar to human. Only the 'Mr' is jarring, conferring a social distinction, and genealogical convention, that is difficult to realize in any aspect of his immediate environment or in the forest habitat that will shortly unfold.

In sum, Milne discovers that we may take great pleasure not only in freeing ourselves of conventional distinctions between humans and animals – and, by the way, in entering a world of abundance among them which is free of consumer production – but also in recognizing that these freedoms are fantasies constructed in images and lines, grounded in iconic work and play. What we recognize as abundance in our habitat depends, his stories tell us, on who we recognize to be inhabiting it, on who else is producing it and us – and the difficult accessibility (its iconic and verbal strangeness pleasurable rather than irksome) of such mundane recognition itself. Even high modernism – with its typically difficult difficulties! – is not always a stranger to this more accessible terrain. We find it in Eliot's illustrated, lyric biographies of cats in *Old Possum's Book of Practical Cats* (1953) – similarly accessible on the face of it, similarly difficult as such. And it is the explicit basis of H.D.'s illustrated *The Hedgehog* (1936), in which the turning point of a girl's growth to maturity is her quest for the meaning of a French word, *hérisson* (hedgehog), which she does not recognize. Such modernist forays, and the complacent anthropocentrism of subject and sign they are able to contest, both persist into contemporary literature and culture, where we are now unfazed by a continual swarm of problem creatures in the totemic iconography of children's culture and commercial signage, across all visual media.

The kind of ambivalence found in Narnia, between an ecology of subjects for which the animal finds wealth in the revelation of habitat, and an anthropocentric sovereignty for which the animal is a produced to be consumed, is not limited to the twilight of the British Empire, nor to Lewis's reactionary Christianity. The same ambivalence is at the heart of perhaps the most influential toy and game phenomenon of the late twentieth century (and still with us), the world of Pokémon produced by Nintendo Co. Ltd, initially as a digital game (1996), and subsequently as a trading-card game, an animé television and movie series, and diverse plastic and plush figures, books, and other collectibles. In the world of Pokémon, children are the 'trainers' of super-powered cute animals that are captured in balls easily stored in their pockets ('Pokémon' is a contraction of the Japanese name 'Pocket Monsters'). These animals can be released from their storage balls to keep company with their trainers or, more frequently to cavort with each other, as the children and animals explore new cityscapes, landscapes, or seascapes. The Pokémon animals are not presented as transcending nature with their powers, like Aslan. Rather, their powers are based on a wide range of natural forces deployed magically – wind, wave, fire, magnetism, electricity, physical force, and even psychological or biophysical drives such as sleep or hunger. With these animals, children inhabit a world of interdependent natural forces, and mastering these forces through the figures of companion animals – in the animé Pokémon, against technological hubris or environmental threat – constitutes a strong ecological message, indeed, an ecology of subjects in the game's fantasy world. 'American kids and parents who become Pokémon collectors and players as well as spectators,' Mark Pizzato has argued in a detailed study of Pokémon and consumer selfhood, 'are drawn to the Japanese cultural connection with nature, with its creatures and spirits, as an iconography within these technological toys and virtual pets. Akin, perhaps, to Shinto animism, and Noh theater, Pokémon presents a mythic world of ghostly forces in natural forms, captured and trained, yet not completely controlled by human characters.'[20] Exploring one's habitat is here a sentimental journey into the wonder of environmental responsibility, made accessible by cuteness. Not only by cuteness, however: also by violence. Child trainers wander in search of new contests between trainers, like child players or traders in real life. In the fantasy contest, each trainer releases his or her Pokémon animals to battle each other with their special powers. All Pokémon games and stories are based on a succession of spectacular, physical and magical battles between creatures, in order that good may conquer evil, while the Pokémon master gains status and power. Non-human animals are nearly completely subservient in this world, while humans are the only masters of other species. In this sense, Pokémon is all about anthropocentric mastery, hierarchical power, and violent competition. Its stories and games use the attraction of an ecology of subjects, and the wondrous modes of language that realize it for children (and those who have been children), only to recontain this ecology in a world of consumer mastery that will neither ruffle actual technocratic optimism, nor compromise the acquisitive or competitive logic of the modern market and its ideals of abundance.

Having your habitat and eating it too, so to speak, as a radical fantasy recontained by consumerism, has flourished in children's and youth culture far beyond Pokémon and its spinoffs. It is there in Tokyo Mew Mew (2000), for example, Mia Ikumi and Reiko Yoshida's popular manga (then animé) series in which felinomorphic girls with special powers battle against environmental villains; or in the American computer game Spore, released by Electronic Arts, Inc. (2008), in which players nurture, grow, and role-play their own invented creatures in fictional habitats, a process based almost entirely on battles for food or dominance, and the acquisition of biophysical traits that will increase power over other species. By

way of contrast, the animé filmmaker Hayao Miyazaki similarly draws on human-animal hybrid figures, plots based on
inter-species relations and environmental threats, and cute
aesthetics, all in the framework of a consumer industry of
spinoff toys and accessories, but with a difference. In his narratives, humans are but fragments, both in their knowledge
and their power, of natural and technological habitats their
subjection to which they must work to learn, and can never
master. Capitalist manufacturing and markets are integrated into the narratives rather than rendered sovereignly invisible – typically as unresolved structures and forces with great
power. In a fine reading of Miyazaki's work, Nathalie op de
Beeck has argued that the child is there evoked not merely as
the embodiment of a radically different perspective, as in the
contemporary examples I have discussed so far, but rather as
a politicized hinge *between* such an alternative perspective and
those of reigning modern ideologies of technological mastery
and consumer production: 'These films explore the betrayal of
children by older generations that would wipe out wild places
and sell off resources for short-term gain; they metaphorical-
ly situate the child between the primeval planet and the corporate economy, and they invite speculation about the basis
for youthful rebellion or alienation in the modern world.'[21]
Interestingly, the same could be said of a very different contemporary text, Philip Pullman's *His Dark Materials* trilogy
of novels (1995–2000; the first novel, retitled *The Golden Com-
pass*, released as a mainstream film in 2001). An epic of parallel realities approaching apocalypse – akin to Lewis's Narnia
series – these stories are about children betrayed by parents
and other adults, who struggle to master cosmic forces to
their conflicting liberal or totalitarian ends. The central figure is a child in whose world the soul of a person, his or her
'daemon,' exists outside their body in the material form of a
talking companion animal. As if in answer to Lewis, the plot
moves against the idea that animal and soul can be divided
– or, indeed, that species may be divided from each other,
and retain the same subjective comprehension. The reward

for such divisive mastery seems to be power and luxurious wealth, but more alluring are the spare lives of the bohemian poor, the 'gyptians,' and of the rustic aliens, the 'mulefa.' Children are the first targets of the villains' biopolitical threat – in the consumerist language of the first novel, to be 'gobbled' – and with the others to help, they do indeed rebel.

Meanwhile, comics artists outside the mainstream have been busy imagining the faces and lives of a utopian world created and re-created only for its habitat wealth. Both Jim Woodring's *Frank* (2004) and Matthew Forsythe's *Ojingogo* (2008) follow strange, stylized creatures – often composites of technological, organic, decorative, and animal form – through surreal sequences of encounters with other beings. In the world of *Frank*, these encounters include familiar human social relations (such as commerce, wage labour, slavery, companionship, hospitality, health care, gifting, theft, and violence), but are more generally enveloped in relations of appropriation and ingestion, transformation and indigestion (see fig. 4.2). The title character has an expression of awe fixed on his goofy face, as if the world is a continual revelation of minor wonders, modulating occasionally to concern or fear as the convoluted, interconnected mortality of his world touches him or his companions. All this transpires in a silent comic, without speech or narration; only faces, bodies, and things united in a vertiginous, plasticity of style. Wealth in such a world is measured by how much one grows sensually among and into the lives of other beings as subjects rather than objects; property has little value other than to mediate such experience.[22] Frank's cryptic utopian life escapes neither violence nor villainy, but it escapes deprivation and loneliness. Forsythe's *Ojingogo* is similarly surreal, and even more minimalist as a world of fragmentary social relations embedded in a strange, ceaseless flow of spatial and bodily involutions, appropriations, and transformations (see fig. 4.3). Both comics try to develop an iconography (style) and iconology (figural identities) that will allow the reader to feel a kind of abundance – sensual fullness, knowledge, physical comfort,

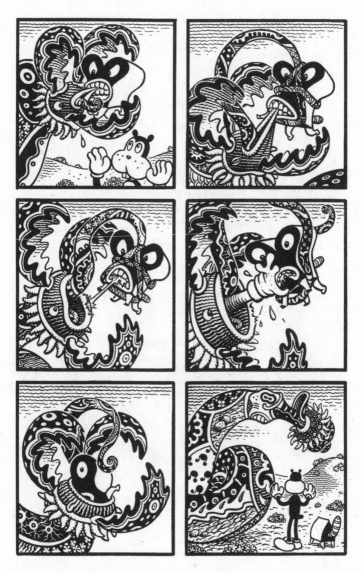

4.2 Jim Woodring, from 'Pushpaw' (1997). From *The Frank Book* (Seattle: Fantagraphics, 2003), p. 183. © 2003 Jim Woodring.

4.3 Matthew Forsythe, from *Ojingogo* (Montreal: Drawn and
Quarterly, 2008). © 2008 Matthew Forsythe.

companionship, and active purpose – as a result of unexpected or even grotesque forms of recognition among species in a habitat writhing with transforming, digestive, productive life at every scale from the microscopic to the immense, only barely human. If utopian, however, neither of these comics looks into the future. Both their worlds are rooted iconologically in the actual otherness of organic lives far removed from human form, like weird fossil creatures or anemones, along with antique or banal technology, like photochemical photography or the fishing rod. The brave new world, these comics suggest, is all around us, if we could only recognize it.

Conclusion

I have argued that modernists and their postmodern creative successors offer great challenges to our economic imaginations. In order to do so, I have drawn from a wide range of differently situated modernisms and habitats, from Europe to North America and Japan, and cast light on commonalities in the folds of individual expression. In diverse forms and styles, and from a variety of planetary sites, these writers and artists have refused a reigning modern ideology of consumer abundance, and have sought to express new kinds of wealth within figures of scarcity. Whether achieved by an exercise of imaginative renunciation and a quest for alternative ways of life, or of imaginative adaptation triggered by a sense of historical rupture, such visions belong to the ambivalent histories of modern primitivism, in which learning to live with less finds so many allegories, and thus remains a needful heritage both for nurture and critique.

Distinguishing four kinds of economic wealth in habitat production, consumer production, welfare production, and natural production, I have endeavoured to show how modernists have striven to distinguish and reveal the diversity of these modes, and especially habitat production, as a radical challenge to a consumer ideology of abundance and scarcity in which the plenitude of habitat is repressed or eclipsed. The representation of habitat production is a project of modernist style, which offers itself as a kind of ascetic withdrawal exercise from consumer desire. Style in this sense will be difficult, not only because it will defy conventional notions of aesthetic or communicative satisfaction, but because it can take on language, verbal or non-verbal, as a resource and process of production itself to be grasped as economic habitat, and nurtured in its plenitude. The high modernists, along with their experimental cousins in popular arts like comics, were able to invent strange, new representational styles in which to unify their visions. The same challenges to economic imagination are found in children's literature, in whose 'accessible difficulty' the modernist project in style is instead realized via forms and genres having deep roots in a didactic heritage in which the recognition of an ecology of subjects is a central theme and is expressed in the normative integration of non-verbal languages of iconology. Indeed, it would seem to be incumbent upon literary studies as a discipline to recognize the iconographic textuality of young children's literature and comics as an unacknowledged form of writing, one that demands different ways of valuing difficulty and practising interpretation.

With the relatively sudden awareness of our small planet as limited in its biophysical resources, hence circumscribed in habitat production, comes a postmodernist twist to the modernist challenge. Re-imagining scarcity is no longer a matter merely of renunciation, and becomes one of adaptation. Nor can consumer production, in this imagined transformation, be fantastically escaped; indeed, in seeking ways to reach others, one might look to some paradoxical transformation of the commodity itself to mediate alternative feelings and practices of wealth.

One might also wear a curious kind of mask, the mask of a distinctively modern animalism. Throughout all these visions, high-art and popular, then and now, run a plethora of human-animal faces and figures which not only reflect a new awareness of the plasticity of the human in the modern age, but more particularly express a post-human continuity with habitat under the unification of a plastic style. These problem creatures are the privileged inhabitants of an alternative economic life with whom we identify, despite their strange, inhuman form, with unaccountable ease. If we can learn to recognize our faces in these iconic mirrors – or, rather, to recognize the significance of our recognizing them – we may open the doors to new structures of economic feeling demanded, in so many different ways, by the artists considered in this book.

There is, I think, a sombre side to our modern love of problem creatures. In the history implied by the life of the small planet, the human species is able to look forward to its own limits, its own likely ends – perhaps sooner, when climate or soil or disease or pollution cannot be mastered, or later, when our sun lives through its own life cycle. In the shadow of every post-human creature with which we seem so eager to identify, there lies perhaps a displaced fear of this death of the human, of the generations of species recognition which enfold all our most profound emotions, collective or intimate. Better to believe we can adapt, evolve beyond this death, and remain one with our habitat, wherever and however produced. Better to cheat – by pretending to affirm – that natural history which we have ultimately failed to annex apart from the history of ourselves. Is it possible that, in a final modernist gesture, we would replace the wish to survive as a triumphant humanity – what was once valued as 'civilization' – with a wish to survive as nothing more than the face of an environment, strictly foreseeable only in the languages of style, a life with a purely aesthetic identity?

Notes

Introduction

1 For reproductions, see Pimenta.

2 *The Tempest*, act 2, scene ii.

3 Foucault, 3–16.

4 Eisenman, 66.

5 Schleifer, on Keynes, 28–9, 26, 29–30; on modernist multiplication, 20 (cf. 24, 52–3, 48). The quotations from Keynes are drawn from his *Essays in Persuasion* (London: Macmillan, 1931), 363, 367.

6 Marsh, 223; on industrialization, 148.

7 Tratner, 98.

8 Keynes quoted in Xenos, 46 (from *Essays in Persuasion*, 369–70). Xenos also notes Marx's programmatic belief in technological advancement to a post-scarcity world, a future of abundance based in the powers of production (even against Malthusian population challenges), a belief that grounds his understanding of historical stages (47–8, 52). Here a powerful future current of Marxist tradition, which Xenos identifies with Herbert Marcuse, dovetails with a now cliché, popular consumerist ideology, that the development of labour-saving, especially automated technology will usher in the possibility of a revolutionary new world of leisure time and satisfactions (53–4).

9 Ekins, 50, 58–60.

10 Eliot, 15.

11 I elsewhere argue that these novels represent the satisfaction of economic activity, and specifically of debt, in terms of gift rather than commodity relations. While this distinction remains within the realm of the type of consumer wealth as I have defined it here, I suggest that it is a devalued economic mode in modern ideology. It also has different consequences than does the market for the other types of wealth here described. See Willmott, *Modernist Goods: Primitivism, the Market, and the Gift*.

12 Eliot, 64–5.

13 The present study does not concern modes of exchange except tangentially. My companion argument for the significance of the gift economy in modernist writing is presented in *Modernist Goods*.

1. Modern Habitats

1 For a reproduction of this first episode of *Little Nemo in Slumberland*, see Canemaker, 98–9. Canemaker includes reproductions of later episodes (4, 104–20) that display the narrative structure of mutation, proliferation, and elimination discussed here.

2 For reproductions of these episodes of *A Pilgrim's Progress*, see Canemaker, 95–6.

3 Stein, *Lectures*, 195–6. On cinematic writing, see 177.

4 Stein, *Three Lives*, 43.

5 Stein, *Three Lives*, 98.

6 Stein, *Last Operas*, 449, 450.

7 Stein, *Lectures*, 54.

8 Stein, *Last Operas*, 473. On Stein's individualism, rentier economic life, and politics, see Hobhouse, 209–11. In this context, 'rentier' refers to a person subsisting on the gains from invested capital. On the rentier basis of modernist culture more generally, see Delany.

9 Nakao and Valenti, 1.

10 Rothkopf, 133.

11 Derrida, 7–8, original emphasis.

12 Klein, 143–6, 165.

13 Murakami quoted in Yoshitake, 125.

14 Murakami, 'Report,' n.pag.

2. Problem Creatures

1 The post-human creature in modernism and postmodernism belongs to the history of modern primitivism. Elsewhere I have discussed the dialectical ambivalence of primitivism, from a left political perspective both conservative and progressive, in the context of modernist expressions of gift and commodity economies (see *Modernist Goods*, esp. 8–13). As illustrated in chapter 2, the same ambivalence underlies the present study.

2 Xenos, 36.

3 Quoted in Xenos, 54–5.

4 Xenos, 95, 85.

5 Wells, *Island of Dr. Moreau*, 141.

6 See Mackenzie and Mackenzie, 125, for the critical reception of this novel.

7 Ray, 36.

8 Lanchester, 107–8; Moore and O'Neill, n.pag.

9 Wells, *War of the Worlds*, 160, 170.

10 Wells, *Island of Dr. Moreau*, 117.

11 Rhys, 149–50, 151–2, 171.

12 Moore, 13–14.

13 Moore, 40.

14 Lawrence, 175.

15 Lawrence, 81–2.

16 Boyle, 78.

17 The list of modernists, excepting Zukovsky, is drawn from Kat historian Bill Blackbeard's introduction to *Krazy & Ignatz*, 6. Zukovsky owned a copy of the Krazy Kat collection for which Cummings had supplied a preface; the copy is in the Harry Ransom Humanities Research Center at the University of Texas. Eliot's appreciation of Herriman is recalled in Levy and Scherle, 47.

18 The literature on Herriman is now extensive; but on race and gender, see Heer, Amiran, and Crocker.

19 Blackbeard, 51.

20 The artwork for this page is reproduced in Varnedoe and Gopnik, 171. For Herriman's interest in Darwinian themes, see also the dodo strip (174) and Heer, 57.

21 See Agamben, *The Open*, 37.

22 McCloud, 32ff.

23 On conventional sweat beads, see McCloud, 130.

24 As these examples testify, such activity is not the sober, industrious, or dutiful labour for consumer production required as a sacrifice to sustain and develop modern wealth. Krazy Kat belongs to the generation of *The Souls of Black Folk* (1903) envisioned by W.E.B. Du Bois, as s/he is marked as black visually and musically (motifs played within strips over the years) and walks along a risky borderline of primitivist racial typage in her joy of productive errantry and modest leisure. Herriman himself has drawn corresponding attention for his mixed-race heritage. For a discussion of race and animal plasticity in modern America, especially in connection with Zora Neale Hurston, see my 'Cat People.'

3. Surviving History

1 Haruki Murakami, *Kafka on the Shore*, 284.

2 This dilemma is given explicit expression in Murakami's reflection on a novel with a similar renunciatory theme and underworld journey plot (*Kafka on the Shore*, 106–7).

3 Haruki Murakami, *Wind-Up Bird*, 603.

4 Nilsen, 16.

5 See Steve Baker's study of Rupert Bear in *Picturing the Beast* for a brilliant reading of the graphic qualities of the Rupert icon and of the graphic animal as a subversive, 'Derridean supplement' working within the talking-animal genre generally (125–39).

6 See Haraway's argument for this general view, 3–42. Her example of a digital image of a tree-stump formation that she names 'Jim's dog,' 5–7, particularly informs my discussion of Nilsen's teddy bear.

7 Nilsen, 41.

8 Ondaatje, 138–9.

9 Ondaatje, 261.

10 Ondaatje, 10.

11 Atwood, *Oryx and Crake*, 10.

12 Atwood, *Oryx and Crake*, 439.

13 Morgan, illustrations facing 137, 136.
14 Patchen, 299.
15 Smith, 157.
16 These three picture-poems are reproduced on the Web page 'Painted and Silkscreened Poems by Kenneth Patchen,' www. concentric.net/~lndb/patchen/patchclr.htm, with the permission of Miriam Patchen. Accessed 8 June 2009.
17 Moore, 48–9.

4. Growing Wonder

1 For modern data and history regarding the 'animalization of children's culture' and language learning, see Melson, 139–43; and Renck, Jalongo, and Brewster, 114.
2 Myers, 3, 16.
3 Renck, Jalongo, and Brewster, 96, 97.
4 In Demers, 10.
5 On romances and animal figures, see Thwaite, 9–11; on the audience of the book in *Don Quixote*, see Part 1, chapter 32 of the novel (Cervantes, 267–8).
6 See Thwaite on one earlier book by Jole (23–4), and popular eighteenth-century illustrated publications of children's verses by Bunyan and by the anonymous T.W. (24). For a selection from Bunyan's book, see Demers, 69–75. For a reproduction from T.W.'s book, see Darton, 58. In all, the everyday life of children is represented as a habitat shared by various other species, domestic and wild.
7 Thwaite, 38.
8 Perrault, 53, 45–6.
9 Quoted in Thwaite, 186.
10 Myers, 83; for further discussion, see 49.
11 Thwaite, 193–4.
12 Kipling, 124.
13 Patten, 46.
14 Lewis, *Horse and His Boy*, 14; *Last Battle*, 193; *Prince Caspian*, 109. On human sovereignty, see also *Prince Caspian*, 64.
15 Milne, 1.

16 Derrida, 107–8.

17 Starting with a cultural studies critique of the British comics icon Rupert Bear (first printed in the 1920s), Steve Baker has made a compatible suggestion to my own in evoking Derrida to argue that hybrid creatures in talking-animal stories are always subversive, more or less explicitly, of conventional categories of the human and the animal, and that the visual representation of such creatures 'has the effect of bringing to light the disruptive potential of the story's animal content' (139).

18 Foucault, 14, 310–11.

19 Milne, 2.

20 Pizzato, 77. The basis of *manga* and *animé* animals in Japanese animist heritages is a common theme in studies of these genres. Compatible with my suggestion that Myers's study of pre-verbal language and subject recognition may be extended to the attraction of animal icons, Pizzato also observes: '[Pokémon] develop greater powers and different forms, yet they have only the syllables of their own names as a language. For example, [the trainer] Ash's favorite pet, Pikachu, can only say: "Pi," "Pika," "Chu," or "Pikachu." In Lacanian terms, Pokémon bear more of the energetic Real and morphing Imaginary orders than Symbolic control. Like small children, they are just starting to learn the Name/No of the Father, in their Symbolic speech and training' (78).

21 op de Beeck, 269.

22 On the desire for property, see especially 'Frank and the Truth about Plenitude,' in Woodring.

Works Cited

Agamben, Giorgio. *Homo Sacer: Sovereign Power and Bare Life.* Trans. Daniel Heller-Roazen. Stanford: Stanford UP, 1998.

– *The Open: Man and Animal.* Trans. Kevin Attell. Stanford: Stanford UP, 2004.

Amiran, Eyal. 'George Herriman's Black Sentence: The Legibility of Race in Krazy Kat.' *Mosaic* 33.3 (Sept. 2000): 57–79.

Atwood, Margaret. *Oryx and Crake.* 2003. Toronto: Random House of Canada (Seal Books), 2004.

Baker, Steve. *Picturing the Beast: Animals, Identity, and Representation.* 2nd ed. Chicago: University of Illinois, 2001.

Blackbeard, Bill, ed. *Krazy & Ignatz.* Seattle: Fantagraphics, 2002.

Boulle, Pierre. *La Planète des singes.* Paris: René Julliard, 1963. Translated into English by Xan Fielding as *Monkey Planet.* London: Secker and Warburg, 1964. Harmondsworth: Penguin, 1966.

Boyle, Kay. *The Crazy Hunter.* New York: New Directions, 1993.

Bunser, A.E. *Macintosh Booth.* Kingston, ON: self-published, 2002.

Canemaker, John. *Winsor McCay: His Life and Art.* 2nd ed. New York: Harry N. Abrams, Inc., 2005.

Cervantes, Miguel de. *Don Quixote.* Trans. Edith Grossman. New York: HarperCollins, 2003.

Coetzee, J.M. *Disgrace.* New York: Vintage, 2000.

Crocker, Elizabeth. '"To He, I Am For Evva True": Krazy Kat's Indeterminate Gender.' *Postmodern Culture* 4.2 (1994).

Darton, F.J. Harvey. *Children's Books in England*. 3rd ed. Revised by Brian Alderson. Cambridge: Cambridge UP, 1982.

Delany, Paul. *Literature, Money and the Market: From Trollope to Amis*. New York: Palgrave Macmillan, 2004.

Demers, Patricia, ed. *From Instruction to Delight: An Anthology of Children's Literature to 1850*. Toronto: Oxford UP, 2004.

Derrida, Jacques. *The Animal That Therefore I Am*. Trans. David Wills. New York: Fordham UP, 2008.

– *Dissemination*. Trans. Barbara Johnson. Chicago: U Chicago P, 1981.

Eisenman, Stephen F. *Gauguin's Skirt*. London: Thames and Hudson, 1997.

Ekins, Paul. *Economic Growth and Environmental Sustainability: The Prospects for Green Growth*. London: Routledge, 2000.

Eliot, T.S. *The Complete Poems and Plays of T.S. Eliot*. London: Faber and Faber, 2004.

Forsythe, Matthew. *Ojingogo*. Montreal: Drawn and Quarterly, 2008.

Foucault, Michel. *The Order of Things: An Archeology of the Human Sciences*. Trans. of *Les Mots et les choses*. New York: Vintage, 1973.

Golding, William. *The Inheritors*. London: Faber and Faber, 1955.

Haraway, Donna. *When Species Meet*. Minneapolis: U of Minnesota P, 2008.

Heer, Jeet. 'Krazy Kat's Colors: The Shadings of George Herriman's Black-and-White World.' *Lingua Franca* 11.6 (Sept. 2001): 53–8.

Hobhouse, Janet. *Everybody Who Was Anybody: A Biography of Gertrude Stein*. London: Weidenfeld and Nicolson, 1975.

Kipling, Rudyard. *The Jungle Book*. London: Macmillan, 1913.

Klein, Naomi. *No Logo: Taking Aim at the Brand Bullies*. Toronto: Vintage, 2000.

Lanchester, Elsa. *Charles Laughton and I*. New York: Harcourt, Brace, and Co., 1938.

Lawrence, D.H. *The Woman Who Rode Away / St. Mawr / The Princess*. London: Penguin, 2006.

Levy, William Turner, and Victor Scherle. *Affectionately, T.S. Eliot: The Story of a Friendship: 1947–1965*. Philadelphia: Lippincott, 1968.

Lewis, C.S. *The Horse and His Boy*. 1954. New York: HarperCollins, 2000.

– *The Last Battle*. 1956. New York: HarperCollins, 2002.

– *The Lion, The Witch and the Wardrobe*. 1950. New York: HarperCollins, 2000.

– *Prince Caspian*. 1951. London: Collins, 1974.

Mackenzie, Norman, and Jeanne Mackenzie. *H.G. Wells: A Biography*. New York: Simon and Schuster, 1973.

Marsh, Alec. *Money and Modernity: Pound, Williams, and the Spirit of Jefferson*. Tuscaloosa: U of Alabama P, 1998.

McCloud, Scott. *Understanding Comics*. New York: HarperPerennial, 1994.

Melson, Gail F. *Why the Wild Things Are: Animals in the Lives of Children*. Cambridge: Harvard UP, 2001.

Milne, A.A. *Winnie-the-Pooh*. Illustrated by E.H. Shepard. 1926. London: Methuen, 1973.

Mizuno, Junko. *Pure Trance*. San Francisco: Last Gasp, 2005.

Moore, Alan (writer), et al. *Saga of the Swamp Thing: Book One*. New York: DC Comics, 2009.

Moore, Alan (writer), and Kevin O'Neill (artist). *The League of Extraordinary Gentlemen, Volume 2*. La Jolla, CA: America's Best Comics, 2003.

Moore, Marianne. *The Complete Poems of Marianne Moore*. Harmondsworth: Penguin, 1982.

Morgan, Richard G., ed. *Kenneth Patchen: A Collection of Essays*. New York: AMS Press, 1977.

Morrison, Grant, et al. *Animal Man: Deus ex Machina*. New York: DC Comics, 2003.

Murakami, Haruki. *Kafka on the Shore*. Translated from the Japanese by Philip Gabriel. New York: Vintage, 2005.

– *The Wind-Up Bird Chronicle*. Translated from the Japanese by Jay Rubin. New York: Vintage, 1998.

Murakami, Takashi. 'Report on the Results of Narumiya Lawsuit,' Kaikai Kiki Co., Ltd. Web page, www.kaikaikiki.co.jp/regarding_the_amicable_settlement. 24 April 2006. Accessed 26 January 2009.

Myers, Gene. *Children and Animals: Social Development and Our Connections to Other Species*. Boulder, CO: Westview P, 1998.

Nakao, Ema, and Kristy Valenti. Interview with Junko Mizuno. *Comics Journal* 273 (2006). Archived on-line at www.tcj.com.

Nilsen, Anders. *Dogs and Water*. Montreal: Drawn and Quarterly, 2007.

Ondaatje, Michael. *The English Patient*. Toronto: McClelland and Stewart, 1992.

op de Beeck, Nathalie. 'Anima and Animé: Environmental Perspectives and New Frontiers in *Princess Mononoke* and *Spirited Away*.' In *The Japanification of Children's Popular Culture: From Godzilla to Miyazaki*. Ed. Mark I. West. Toronto: Scarecrow P, 2009.

Patchen, Kenneth. *The Journal of Albion Moonlight*. New York: New Directions, 1941.

Patten, Fred. 'The Allure of Anthropomorphism in *Animé* and *Manga*.' In *The Japanification of Children's Popular Culture: From Godzilla to Miyazaki*. Ed. Mark I. West. Toronto: Scarecrow P, 2009. 41–52.

Perrault, Charles. *The Complete Fairy Tales of Charles Perrault*. Trans. Neil Philip and Nicoletta Simborowski. New York: Clarion, 1993.

Pimenta, Rui. *Living within the Means of Existence*. Exhibition pamphlet. Ottawa: Karsh-Masson Gallery (City of Ottawa), 2009.

Pizzato, Mark. 'Pokémon as Theater: Training the Pocket Monsters of Self and Consumerism.' In *The Japanification of Children's Popular Culture: From Godzilla to Miyazaki*. Ed. Mark I. West. Toronto: Scarecrow P, 2009.

Ray, Gordon. *H.G. Wells and Rebecca West*. New Haven: Yale UP, 1974.

Renck, Melissa Ann, Mary Renck Jalongo, and Jeffrey C. Brewster. 'Companion Animals in Books: Themes in Children's Literature.' In *The World's Children and Their Companion Animals: Developmental and Educational Significance of the Child/Pet Bond*. Ed. Mary Renck Jalongo. Olney, MD: Association for Childhood Education International, 2004.

Rhys, Jean. *Tigers Are Better-Looking: With a Selection from The Left Bank*. Harmondsworth: Penguin, 1972.

Rothkopf, Scott. 'Takashi Murakami: Company Man.' In Takashi Murakami, ©*Murakami*. Los Angeles: Museum of Contemporary Art / New York: Rizzoli International, 2008.

Schleifer, Ronald. *Modernism and Time: The Logic of Abundance in Literature, Science, and Culture, 1880–1930*. Cambridge: Cambridge UP, 2000.

Smith, Larry R. *Kenneth Patchen*. Boston: G.K. Hall and Co., 1978.

Stein, Gertrude. *Last Operas and Plays*. Ed. Carl Van Vechten. New York: Vintage, 1975.

– *Lectures in America*. Boston: Beacon, 1957.

– *Three Lives and Q.E.D.* Ed. Marianne DeKoven. New York: W.W. Norton, 2006.

Thwaite, M.F. *From Primer to Pleasure: An Introduction to the History of Children's Books in England, from the Invention of Printing to 1900.* London: Library Association, 1963.

Tratner, Michael. *Deficits and Desires: Economics and Sexuality in Twentieth-Century Literature.* Stanford: Stanford UP, 2001.

Varnedoe, Kirk, and Adam Gopnik. *High and Low: Modern Art and Popular Culture.* New York: Museum of Modern Art, 1990.

Wells, H.G. *The Island of Dr. Moreau.* A Critical Text of the 1896 London First Edition, with an Introduction and Appendices. Ed. Leon Stover. Jefferson, NC, and London: McFarland and Co., 1996.

– *The War of the Worlds.* Ed. Martin A. Danahay. Peterborough, ON: Broadview P, 2003.

Willmott, Glenn. 'Cat People.' *Modernism/Modernity* 27.4 (2010): 839–56.

– *Modernist Goods: Primitivism, the Market, and the Gift.* Toronto: U of Toronto P, 2008.

Woodring, Jim. *The Portable Frank.* Seattle: Fantagraphics, 2008.

Xenos, Nicholas. *Scarcity and Modernity.* London: Routledge, 1989.

Yoshitake, Mika. 'The Meaning of the Nonsense of Excess.' In Takashi Murakami, ©*Murakami*. Los Angeles: Museum of Contemporary Art / New York: Rizzoli International, 2008.

Index